A Guide to Understanding International Trade and the Balance of Payments: Everything You Need to Intelligently Formulate and Evaluate Public Policy Proposals

Gail E. Makinen, Ph.D.
Retired Adjunct Professor
McCourt School of Public Policy
Georgetown University
Washington, DC

Dedication

My interest in International Economics has persisted for more than half a century. It was set in motion by two of the most inspiring teachers it was my good fortune to know. The first was Michael O'Connor who, when I was an undergraduate, ignited my interests in this field. He helped me secure a National Defense Act fellowship that permitted me to go to graduate school. During my years as a graduate student I was fortunate to have as a teacher H. Peter Gray, who continued to inspire me in this field, who supervised both my M.A. thesis and my Ph.D. dissertation, and with whom I published the first academic paper to bear my name, in the *Journal of Business*. Over subsequent years he not only continued to be my mentor, but we became close friends. To both of these fine gentlemen and wonderful teachers, I dedicate this book. I wish they had lived long enough to have seen their handiwork in its pages.

Acknowledgements

This book is the distillation of a series of lectures I gave over an 11-year period as an adjunct professor at what is now known as the McCourt School of Public Policy at Georgetown University. Most of the students in my classes had a limited background in both macro- and microeconomic theory or had taken these courses some years earlier as undergraduates. The winner of the 2011 Nobel Prize in Economics, Professor Thomas Sargent, observed that "economics is organized common sense." I intended to prove that this is true. Simple notions often have profound implications for public policy, and so it is with international economics. To this end, I condensed a good part of my course in international economics to prove that Professor Sargent is correct. If I have failed, it is no reflection on him.

A book is seldom completed without the help of numerous people. I would like to thank the many students I taught at the McCourt School who provided me with an unexpected pleasure late in my professional life. Leonard Berman, Kent Weaver, Kerry Pace, Leslie Evertz, Eric Gardner and, especially our energetic and inspiring dean, Judy Feder, made this opportunity possible and the experience memorable.

A debt is always incurred in writing books to a number of people who give their time and opinions on what you have written and make suggestions for how it might be improved. I have been blessed with such a debt. It is owed to Thomas Woodward, Bill Bomberger, Kurt Schuler, Marc Labonte, and Mark Bernkopf, who have also been longtime friends and, in several instances, my colleagues and co-authors. I would also like to thank Amy Schuler for a fine editing job, Lilly Winfree for technical assistance, Pam Holland for her artistic efforts, the late Robert Anderson for obtaining crucial data, and Sue Ellen Sherblom for her magnificent cover design. As always, any errors are mine.

One of my graduate school teachers was Abba Lerner. When I returned to teaching, I reread his sadly neglected paper published in 1936 entitled "The Symmetry between Import and Export Taxes." It substantially influenced the way I now think about public policy issues involving international trade and finance. I regret having overlooked it for so many years.

Contents

I. Introduction

The economic performance of a nation is judged by a number of statistical measures. Popular among these is how much it produces (its gross domestic product or GDP), its unemployment rate, and the stability of its price level (its rate of inflation). Almost no nation exists in total isolation, so another performance measure relates to its exchange of goods, services, and financial assets with other nations (its balance-of-payments accounts). In fact, to compute its GDP accounts it must be able to compute these values. The following narrative is related to this measure of economic performance, and as an introduction to this discussion, the history of the American balance of payments since 1970 is displayed on the next page in Figure 1.

These data are unprecedented in one sense: They show that beginning in 1980, except for one year, the balance of payments has been consistently negative. No comparable period can be found in the recorded history of the United States. The persistence and magnitude of this deficit have not passed unnoticed. It has been of growing concern to economists, politicians, and the public in general. Too many well-known American economists have declared during this period that the situation just couldn't continue, and they now know that they were embarrassingly wrong. It has continued and is highly likely to continue for the foreseeable future. Something must be wrong with the thinking of these esteemed persons as well as political leaders and the casual observer. This humble effort is to explain what we should know about international trade and finance in order to understand why this has occurred, what its effects have been, and what the consequences are likely to be should it continue. On this basis, a clear course for sound public policy decisions can be set out. As a prelude to this discussion, one conclusion is that this long string of trade deficits is not a sign of weakness. Quite the contrary, a case can be made that it is a sign of strength. Note also that this shift to a prolonged period of balance of payments deficits is coincident with the shift in exchange rate regimes. Beginning in the early 1970s, the United States moved from a fixed to a flexible exchange rate regime. What role, if any, did this play in the persistent deficits?

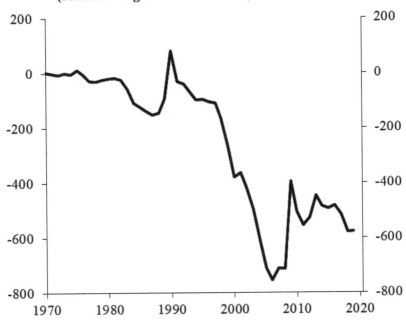

Figure 1
Balance of Payments of the United States 1970-2019
(balance on goods and services, billions of dollars)

Source: Bureau of Economic Analysis, U.S. Department of Commerce

A. How Important Is Trade to the United States?

The journey to understanding the balance of payments begins by understanding the underlying data. The figure above gives some information about the absolute size of the deficit but tells us little about its relative importance. For this, we compare the size of the deficit to the nominal value of GDP. For the decade 1970 to 1980, it varied within a range of +1 percent and -1 percent of GDP; from 1980 to 1990, the range was from 0 percent to -3.3 percent of GDP; and from 1991 onward, it has varied within a range of 0 percent to -6.6 percent of GDP. The overall trend since 1990 has been downward — the trade deficit has been a growing percentage of GDP.

The next step in assessing the importance of the data is to ascertain how open the American economy is or how large the foreign trade sector is relative to the total domestic output of goods and services. A widely used measure of openness is obtained by dividing the sum of the goods and services exported and imported by the total value of GDP or $((X + M)/GDP)$. Using this measure tells us that the U.S. economy has become increasingly open since the post-World War II period. In 1960, the sum of exports and imports was 9.6 percent of GDP. This increased to 10.9 percent in 1970, rose to about 20.0 percent in both 1980 and 1990 and then increased, but remained nearly stationary at about 26.0 percent for 2000, 2010 and 2019.

The increasing openness of the world economy or, as the popular press calls it, the increasing complexity of foreign source supply chains, complicates the calculation of openness as well as the analysis of who bears the burden of some public policy choices.

In the period before World War II, most of the nation's exports were produced primarily by domestic labor and capital. To be sure, some exports may have contained inputs that were obtained abroad. As the world economy has become increasingly integrated, a larger and larger portion of exports have come to include a foreign component. With this, the value of imports is counted twice in the numerator of the formula used to measure openness. It is counted once as an import and again to the extent that it is included in a country's exports. For example, the U.S. exports a large amount of component parts for motor vehicles to Canada where they are assembled and sent back to the U.S. The full market value of those exports will enter the U.S. balance of payments. When the parts are assembled in Canada and the motor vehicles exported to the United States, the market value of these vehicles (the cost of the parts and to assemble the vehicles in Canada) will be recorded by the U.S. as an import. Thus, the value of the numerator contains both the U.S export of the components and the value of those components in their assembled form that are subsequently imported by the U.S.

The denominator of the measure of openness is not affected by this problem since in computing GDP, imports used to produce U.S. output are subtracted from that output to arrive at the value of domestically produced output.

Thus, the increasing openness of the world economy since the end of World War II may not be quite as it appears. Some portion, and an increasingly larger portion, may be due to the way we calculate openness. It should be noted that this problem is well understood and work is in progress to develop export and import data that contain only domestic value added. This means that in the computations above, the value of Canadian assembled vehicles imported to the U.S. would be valued by the U.S. at only their assembly costs (or domestic value added) in Canada.

Of far more importance is the public policy implication of the increasing percentage of imports whose content comes from third countries. The U.S., as well as other nations, has not been reluctant to use tariffs (taxes on imports) and other trade impediments to force its foreign policy objectives on other nations. Underlying these policies is a belief that the entire value of the import is made in the country that is the object of the trade impediment. With the growing importance of global supply chains, this is very unlikely. It is estimated, for example, that at least half of Chinese exports to the U.S. have a large third country origin. This is particularly true of Chinese electronics exports to the U.S. While the label they bear says "made in China," this is only partially true. What the Chinese often do is assemble the parts made elsewhere. Since the U.S. tariff applies to the entire product, not just the Chinese value added, the U.S. trade war is waged against third countries with whom the U.S. has no problems or who may even be allies of the U.S., such as Japan. U.S. foreign policy based on trade impediments may have the unintended consequence of antagonizing our allies and major trading partners with whom we have no difficulties.

We are now about to begin the main part of our discussion, and it is at this point that it would be useful to state its major conclusions. First, in the absence of the net international movement of capital, the goods and services exported by a country must be equal to the imports of that country. Thus, any public policy action that affects imports will affect exports to the same degree. Second, how this will happen will depend on the international exchange-rate regime in place when the action is taken. Third, for a country to have an international trade deficit it must be a net importer of capital and for this to happen, its domestic saving must be less than its domestic investment. Any attempt to deal with the trade deficit that does not address the domestic saving-investment imbalance of a country is doomed to failure.

To deal in part with the first conclusion, it will be necessary to see what the United States exports and imports and with whom we trade. By looking at this with a historical perspective, we will see the changing patterns of trade and the changing importance of our trading partners. It will be useful to remember that other countries experience the same changes, and their changes will affect us in the same way. In some instances, these changes will affect our domestic sectors in ways that are uncomfortable, in the sense that the output of these sectors will have to contract and the labor and capital once employed will have to be transferred. The same is true for technological changes. These, however, we seem to bear better than if they originate abroad.

Table 1
Composition of U.S. Exports and Imports, 1960-2019
(percent of total)

	Exports		Imports	
	Goods	**Services**	**Goods**	**Services**
1960	76	24	65	35
1970	75	25	73	27
1980	82	18	86	14
1990	72	28	81	19
2000	72	28	85	15
2010	69	31	82	18
2019	65	35	81	19

Source: Bureau of Economic Analysis, U.S. Department of Commerce

B. What Does the U.S. Trade?

The exports and imports of the United States have undergone a profound change over the 400 years since European settlers first arrived on these shores. In 1860, on the eve of the Civil War, nearly 75 percent of U.S. exports consisted of raw materials, with cotton accounting for half our exports alone. An almost identical percentage of American imports were of a manufactured nature. As shown in Tables 1 and 2, profound changes have occurred in the composition of U.S. trade. Given the magnitude of these changes, the world economy has had to make substantial adjustments to how and what we produce and we to similar changes abroad. It is important to keep in mind that similar things are going on in other countries and they have implications for policies in this country.

Table 2
Part A: Composition of Exports (percent of total)

	Agri-culture	Industrial Supplies and Materials	Capital Goods	Auto-motive	Consumer and All Other Goods
1980	19	29	34	8	10
1990	10	25	40	9	16
2000	7	21	46	10	16
2010	9	30	35	9	17
2019	8	32	34	10	16

Part B: Composition of Imports (percent of total)

	Petro-leum	Industrial Supplies and Materials	Capital Goods	Auto-motive	Consumer and All Other Goods
1980	32	21	13	11	23
1990	13	17	24	16	30
2000	10	15	28	16	31
2010	18	14	23	12	33
2019	7	21	24	16	32

Source: Bureau of Economic Analysis, U.S. Department of Commerce

Often overlooked in the discussion of foreign commerce is that the U.S. buys from foreigners and sells to them a wide range of financial assets: stocks, bonds, and mortgages, as well as physical assets. These also appear in the balance of payments. Later we will see that the balance of trade deficit shown in Figure 1 is balanced by a net outflow of American financial assets meaning that the U.S. is the net recipient of foreign investment. The data in Table 1 reveal another important trend in the composition of U.S. exports: the growing importance of services. Over the past 50 years they have grown from about a quarter of U.S. exports to more than a third. Similarly, their import share has fallen by nearly one-half. Included in services are those related to transportation, travel, education, insurance, finance, the use of intellectual property, information, consulting, legal, and so on.

Since the trade in goods dominates both exports and imports over the past half century, the data shown in Table 2 will give us a better notion of what is included in that category. Surprisingly, the U.S. remains an exporter of agricultural products. A large part of this is still cotton. U.S. exports continue to be dominated by manufactured goods. We have not become a nation of "hamburger flippers." They also show the effect of the fracking revolution in the extraction of oil that has caused a dramatic decline in the proportion of imports accounted for by petroleum products.

Our imports of goods appear to be heavily concentrated in automotive and consumer and other goods (here agricultural products are to be found). An important component in consumer goods is electronics.

C. With Whom Does the U.S. Trade?

The eight major trading partners of the United States, measured by both exports and imports, and the relative importance of each, are listed in Table 3.[1]

The first thing to note is that this is not trade between an industrial country and less-developed countries. America and most of its major trading partners are at a similar state of development. Second, since 2007, the sum of Canadian and Mexican trade has accounted for about 33 percent of U.S. exports and 27 percent of U.S imports. Such a large volume of trade was one of the reasons why it made sense to try and create a single trading area: hence the rationale for the North American Free Trade Agreement (NAFTA) created in the late 1990s (and continued in the United States-Mexico-Canada Agreement [USMCA] of 2019). Third has been the growing importance of trade with China. While U.S. exports to China have accounted for roughly 6 percent to 7½ percent of total U.S. exports, imports from China have accounted for about 15 percent to nearly 22 percent of all U.S. imports. This imbalance has drawn the attention of many American policymakers. The causes of this imbalance and the proposals for remediation will be analyzed later in this text.

---

[1] The data in both Tables 1 and 2 are subject to the caveat noted above about double counting.

Table 3
Leading Trading Partners of the United States, 2007 and 2019
(percent of total)

	2007		2019	
	Exports	**Imports**	**Exports**	**Imports**
Canada	20.3	16.2	17.8	12.8
Mexico	11.7	10.4	15 6	14.3
United Kingdom	4.6	2.8	4.2	2.5
France	2.1	2.1	2.3	2.3
Germany	4.2	4.5	3.7	5.1
China	5.7	15.1	6.5	18.1
Japan	5.3	10.4	4.5	5.7
South Korea	2.7	2.5	3.5	3.1
TOTAL	**56.6**	**63.8**	**64.6**	**69.6**

Source: Bureau of Economic Analysis, U.S. Department of Commerce

This table also draws our attention to the fact that trade is not a simple two-way exchange, but part of a matrix involving many countries — who at the same time are trading with each other. Many commentators like to focus on the trade balance with a particular country, often suggesting that something is amiss if imports and exports are significantly asymmetric. But it is worth emphasizing that such a situation can be common and natural and says nothing about trade overall because there are other trading partners with whom the reverse may be true. If anything is to be learned from looking at the balance of trade, one must look at the whole and not get caught up in meaningless observations about its isolated parts.

D. Contending Doctrines on the Benefits of Trade: Mercantilism

The international trade policies of governments today are not new. The major contending doctrines underpinning those policies have a long and historic origin. For convenience, if not fact, economists and historians break them down into two periods: 1500-1800, and 1800 to the present.

The first was given the name **Mercantilism** while the latter has been associated with **Free Trade.**[2]

The Mercantilist period coincides with the formation and growth of the national state, primarily in Europe, and England in particular. The policy that emerged was designed to create and enhance the economic foundation of the state and might be thought of as an early and primitive example of what we now call an "industrial policy," or one in which government plays an important role in picking winners and losers. Manufacturing was usually on the top of the winners list, and it was given special attention. This involved government grants of monopolies to produce goods and services and exploit various geographic areas; tariffs, quotas, and subsidies to encourage the development of export- and import-substitute industries; forbidding the export of certain technologies and capital goods; fixing wages and prices; and the use of the armed forces to acquire and secure colonial possessions, especially if they contained valuable raw material resources or commanded strategic transit routes. In essence, the policy was highly nationalistic and represented the views of producers.

This industrial policy had a rather curious view about the conduct of and benefits from trade. The international exchange of goods and services was not seen as mutually beneficial. Rather, only the seller gained from trade, and the nation should strive through its industrial policy to manage or control trade to produce the largest trade surplus possible, (or in the words of the day, a "favorable balance of trade"). Hence, (English) government trade policy was to be guided, according to Thomas Mun, an important executive in the British East India Company (the mega-trading company of its day), by a simple rule: **we must sell more to strangers yearly than we consume of theirs in value.**[3] In effect, a balance of payments surplus was viewed as a businessman would view profit, while a deficit would be viewed as a loss. To people like Thomas Mun, the U.S. data in Figure 1 would suggest the abject failure of government trade policy.

---

[2] For a comprehensive discussion of this subject, see Douglas A. Irwin, *Against the Tide: An Intellectual History of Free Trade* (Princeton, N.J.: Princeton University Press. 1996).

[3] Mun's slim treatise of 88 pages is entitled *England's Treasure by Forreign Trade or The Balance of Our Forreign Trade is the Rule of Our Treasure* (1664).

Why was the focus of trade policy on the attainment of a positive trade balance? Various explanations have been forthcoming. But it shouldn't be overlooked that this policy goal was not attainable for each country as collectively they could not simultaneously all have a trade surplus. Attempts to do so contributed to a good deal of international tension and military activity. A popular explanation for this goal is that it would lead to a net inflow of money — which meant gold and silver — and this would enhance the wealth of the nation as it would a great merchant. Other explanations that have been suggested include: (1) the trade surplus provided a continuous stimulus to aggregate demand and employment; (2) the inflow of money lead to low interest rates that both encouraged capital formation and reduced or kept low production costs; (3) it augmented the "wage fund," making increased employment possible; and (4) it provided the wherewithal to fight foreign wars.[4]

E. The Free Trade Counterattack

Two forces arose to attack this industrial policy. The first was practical and due to some serious fault lines or internal inconsistencies in the package of policies that its proponents and supporters recommended. The second was intellectual and laid the foundations for the new trade policy paradigm.

Policy fault lines. The industrial policy of controlled trade was not harmonious. The grant of monopolies, for example, precluded many individuals from entering various lines of business, causing internal strife and inefficient production that might not have taken place with competition. Manufacturers and exporters favored low tariffs on food imports so that they could pay low wages and be competitive, whereas the land-owning class favored tariffs that kept food prices high as this meant a higher rent from their land. The paucity of law enforcement and the profits accruing to monopolists encouraged smuggling, and with this came a general disregard for the law as well as the bribing of public officials to obtain monopolies and other favors in trade. The use of tariffs for

---

[4] Amazingly, the famous British economist John Maynard Keynes included in his magnum opus, the *General Theory of Employment, Interest, and Money* (1936), a chapter on Mercantilism and viewed favorably the arguments of the early formulators and proponents of this industrial policy — they were the precursors of some of the views he supported in his book.

protection reduced the principal revenue source of the government, while subsidies diverted resources from other pressing needs. As economic theory became more sophisticated, the argument against this system tended to be framed in terms of the dead-weight losses (or losses for which there are no offsetting benefits) associated with tariffs, quotas, and subsidies.

The intellectual attack. Beginning in the mid-18th and early 19th centuries there had been rumblings of intellectual discontent with the system of controlled trade. The main intellectual assault was the product of three men; two Scots, David Hume and Adam Smith, and an Englishman, David Ricardo. Their work was done over the period from 1752 to 1817. They provided an intellectual basis that not only explained why focusing trade policy on obtaining a continuous positive trade balance was fruitless, but set out the theoretical foundation for an alternative paradigm that both explained the benefits of trade to a country and the determinants of its exports and imports. It was international in scope, emphasized the efficient allocation of resources, represented the views of consumers, and saw trade as mutually beneficial – both parties to an exchange gained.

F. David Hume

David Hume was a lawyer and philosopher who came somewhat late in life to the study of economics. His great contribution was to show that no nation can continuously have an excess of exports over imports; in more modern jargon, "this is not a steady-state solution." He made this contribution in 1752 in a short pamphlet entitled *An Essay on Money*. The ideas in this essay had been around for some time. It was Hume's contribution to pull them together and relate them to the balance of payments doctrine of the Mercantilists.

Hume began with the relationship between the amount of money in a country and the level of its prices. The relationship is positive. The larger the amount of money relative to the amount of goods and services, the higher their prices will be individually and hence the average level of all prices. The opposite will occur if the amount of money is smaller or reduced.

Let us begin, he said, with a world in which trade is balanced for each country. Let one country, called HOME, impose a tax on imports to achieve a favorable (or positive) balance of trade. Assume that HOME is successful, and it now exports more than it imports. The resultant favorable trade balance means that there will be a net inflow of money from FOREIGN to HOME. The net inflow of money to HOME will cause its price level to rise and cause the price level of FOREIGN to fall. This change in relative prices will change consumer behavior. The consumers in HOME will switch from their own goods and services to the substitutes produced in FOREIGN and the consumers in FOREIGN will switch from buying the goods and services of HOME to their own substitutes. As a result, the net exports of HOME will fall and continue to fall until trade is once again balanced. This switching will come to an end when the price levels in the two countries bear the same relationship that they bore before the imposition of the tariff. All that will have been accomplished is that the total amount of world trade will have declined: Each country will export less than before. This method of restoring equilibrium to the balance of payments is called the **Price-Specie Flow Mechanism,** and it remains a key component of how the gold standard (and other monetary arrangements in which the nominal exchange rate is fixed) works to restore equilibrium in the face of an economic shock.

Before continuing, how would Hume explain the data depicted in Figure 1? They show a long-time U.S. trade deficit so long and so large that it would suggest that the United States would run out of money with no equilibrium in sight. We will return to this topic later, and at that time we will see what Hume has to say.

G. Adam Smith

Adam Smith had several occupations. He was primarily a professor at both the Universities of Edinburgh and Glasgow, Scotland. For several years, he also held the official position of Collector of Customs for Scotland. He is regarded as the founding father of modern economics. In 1776 he published his monumental work *An Inquiry into the Nature and Causes of the Wealth of Nations.* A major part of this book was intended as an attack on what he called the "mercantile" system meaning the economic system then instituted and embraced by the British government. It is from this word that Mercantilist is derived.

Smith attacked Mercantilism on several fronts. The first was a broad-based philosophical attack on the systems' subordination of the individual to the state, giving rise to the suggestion that his book might be subtitled "Free to Choose." Smith argued that individuals should be free to choose the profession or occupation they entered, to produce any (lawful) goods and services that individuals might find useful, to exchange goods and services with others regardless of where these individuals might live, and free to determine how to allocate their savings among alternative investments, etc.

Some argued that this freedom to choose would lead to an unstable economy in which prices would not converge but fluctuate wildly. Smith's observations taught him that individuals were quite capable of the most complex type of economic reasoning and activity and that this individual action was not unstable in the aggregate. That is, without guidance from the government, individual economic action led to a stable system. This is no doubt because of his belief that individuals in pursuit of their own self-interest would be guided by an **invisible hand** to promote the best interest of society.

Smith's economic attack on Mercantilism was several-fold. First, he implicitly accepted Hume's argument that it is pointless to try to continuously export more than you imported: This will come to nothing in the end, as the market will determine the flow of money to each country such that their price levels will produce balanced trade among them. Second, he argued that the end purpose of economic activity is not production per se, employment per se, or exports per se, but the standard of living and this involves consumption — the amount and variety of goods and services available. And this can best be achieved by minimizing state control of the economy and opening it to **free trade**. It should be noted that by *free trade* Smith meant "the absence of import barriers and export subsidies." A government might still interfere with trade on "moral" grounds (slave trade), "public health" grounds (drug trade, arms trade), and "national security" grounds (Navigation Acts); to tax imports at the same rate as imposed on domestic competing goods, etc.[5] Thus tariffs may be necessary for a state to function, even one that practices free trade.

---

[5] Smith conceded that a nation may use tariffs on both imports and exports to finance the proper functions of government. Tariffs on imports were an important source of U.S. federal revenue. On the eve of the Civil War in 1860, they accounted for 90 percent of federal tax revenue.

G.1. How Does Free Trade Contribute to a Higher Standard Living?

(1) It increases the variety of goods and services that are available to satisfy the needs and wants of individuals. In the words of Smith: "It expands the sum of enjoyments." Thus, trade is mutually beneficial. All parties to the transaction gain.

(2) It ensures that only efficient production survives. In this sense, it ensures that capital and labor will be efficiently allocated. Thus, given the resources of the world maximum output will be forthcoming (note the international perspective of this argument: World output is maximized).

(3) It expands the size of the market and this enables economies of scale to be realized, reducing costs of production and increasing the amount of goods and services that can be produced from given resources. In Smith's words: the degree of specialization is limited by the size of the market. Notice this possibility of expanding the size of the market works to the advantage of small countries whose domestic markets may limit their ability to achieve possible scale economies.

If free trade prevailed, what would determine where production would take place and what would be exchanged internationally? According to Smith, countries would export those goods and services that they produced more cheaply (as measure in terms of labor time) than other countries and import goods and services that other countries produced at a lower labor cost per unit than they did. Price would govern the patterns of trade because it would reflect the cost of production that, in turn, would reflect the efficiency of its production. To put it another way, countries would export those goods and services which they produced most efficiently and import those goods and services produced most efficiently abroad. This we call the theory of **Absolute Advantage.**[6]

G.2. The Problem with Smith's Theory

Some countries may have no good or service in which they are the low-cost producer. That is, they cannot produce any good or service more efficiently than other countries. Smith suggests that there would be countries that only imported goods and services and exported nothing. Since we don't observe such countries, something other than **Absolute Advantage** must explain trade.

---

[6] Smith's and Ricardo's theory of value is explained in Appendix A.

Table 4
Ricardo's Trade Example

	Wine	Cloth
HOME	20	60
FOREIGN	10	20

H. David Ricardo

The third great contributor to the case for free trade was a stockbroker and ultimately a member of the British parliament, David Ricardo. In 1817, he published his seminal work *Principles of Political Economy and Taxation*, a portion of which dealt with international trade

The international trade theory developed by Ricardo was to serve two purposes. First, it resolved the problem in Smith's model that arises when a country has no good or service that it produces more efficiently than any other. Ricardo showed that even should this situation arise, a mutually beneficial trade can still occur between countries. Second, he shows that not only is trade mutually beneficial, but it is possible to quantify the static gains from trade.

Ricardo did these two things using a very simple and clever example shown as Table 4. He assumed there were two countries that produced two products — cloth and wine. For reasons not specified one country HOME is more efficient in the production of both products. According to Smith, trade would not be possible between the two countries since FOREIGN, the high-cost producer of both products, would have nothing to export. Not so, says Ricardo. A mutually advantageous exchange will emerge since in the absence of trade in HOME, three cloth will exchange for one wine whilst in FOREIGN two cloth will exchange for one wine. Since relative pre-trade prices are different, it will be mutually advantageous for both to trade. HOME will gain if it can acquire one wine by giving up less than three cloth and FOREIGN will gain if it can acquire more than two cloth for each wine it gives up.

Who will specialize in what? As viewed by Ricardo, each country will specialize in the production and export of the good in which it is either most efficient or least inefficient or, in which it has the greatest **comparative advantage** or **least comparative disadvantage**. In the case in point, HOME will specialize in cloth and FOREIGN wine. Notice, each country will be completely specialized. It will only produce one product and import the other. It will not have an importing competing industry.

Where will the international exchange rate settle? First, it must settle within the two respective pre-trade barter rates. That is, 1 wine = 3 cloth and 1 wine = 2 cloth. Where, within this range, depends on the relative intensity of demand of one country for the good of the other. If HOME's demand for cloth is great, but FOREIGN's for wine is weak, the exchange rate will be near 1 wine for 3 cloth and the opposite if FOREIGN has the more intense desire.

The exchange rate that is finally established is known in the literature as the "**real exchange rate,**" or "**commodity terms of trade,**" or the "**net barter terms of trade.**" It must have one characteristic. It must ensure that trade is balanced between the two countries. The real exchange rate is discussed in greater detail later.

I. What Have We Learned from This Trio?

Hume, Smith, and Ricardo, in developing the foundation of the new industrial policy based on free trade, have much to teach us as we think about and formulate sound public policy. A sample would include:

(1) While **Absolute Advantage** has shortcomings in explaining trade patterns between nations, it can be used to make a statement about the standard of living of the two countries. Since the workers in HOME are from two to three times more productive than those in FOREIGN, they will enjoy a higher standard of living and it will be from 2 to 3 times as high.

(2) **Is trade always mutually advantageous (as measured in Ricardian terms)?** The answer is usually "yes" unless the countries are of quite different size in terms of labor force. The reason this is somewhat important is that if one country is small, it could become specialized before the other. And should this occur, it must trade at the price ratio prevailing in the larger country before trade – it enjoys all the gains as measured by Ricardo. At the least, neither country in this example is made worse off.

(3) **Will trade cause a redistribution of income in either country or, will we have winners and losers?** The answer is no. In each country, after trade begins, all the labor in one sector will be moved to the sector in which the country has either the comparative advantage or least comparative disadvantage. Since the labor in both sectors before trade were paid the same real wage, the shift will leave their real wage unaltered;

they will produce the same number of units as the labor in that sector (i.e., in the jargon of the economists, the marginal product of labor is unaffected by the transfer). Will this cause a redistribution of income or do we have winners and losers? The answer is no. This is due to three reasons. First, labor is homogeneous. Second, before trade it was paid the same real wage in both sectors. Third, when it is moved it does not alter the marginal product in the sector it is moved to. Because this is the case, it will be paid the same real wage as the workers in that sector which is the same real wage it was paid in the sector it came from. However, all workers will share in the gains from trade and in that sense the real income of all will rise. The Ricardian world is nice in this sense. Trade only creates winners.

(4) Money. While money and the market exchange rate have not yet been introduced in this discussion, it will be an appropriate time now to do so indirectly. We know that the real exchange rate must be the same in both countries (for example, 2.4 wine = 1 cloth) after trade. But this is a relative price. The question now becomes: Must the market exchange rate be such that the absolute price of the goods is the same in each country? Or, will the Big Mac sell for the same price in both countries when their currencies are converted to a common currency using the market exchange rate? Hume tells us that the answer is yes. Unless this is the case, sellers will buy where the Big Mac is cheaper and sell it where it is higher. And this arbitrage will continue until the two money prices are the same.

(5) Money wage equality? Given that the absolute or money price of cloth and wine must be the same in both countries after trade, will the money wage in each also be the same? No. The difference in money wages must reflect the underlying real wage difference and that depends on the productivity differences.

(6) Trade and immigration. Is trade a substitute for the movement of the factor of production in raising the real wage of labor in FOREIGN? That is, if I want to raise the real wage of labor in the world, would it be better to permit immigration in place of free trade? The answer has some complexity to it. A simple answer would be yes. A movement of labor from FOREIGN to HOME would magically improve the productivity of FOREIGN's labor and the real wage of these immigrants would then be equal to the real wage of HOME's labor. However, if FOREIGN could trade with HOME at the price ratio prevailing in HOME before trade, it would accomplish much the same end, but this is unlikely. Thus, if higher real wages are the goal, the free movement of labor is preferable to free trade.

23

(7) Suggests additional research. The Ricardian trade model produces complete product specialization per country (meaning there will be no import-competing product and this holds even if more than two countries and two commodities are introduced). A country will not export and import the same thing, but this conclusion appears to be contradicted by data both for the U.S. and many other countries. From the data given above, the U.S. appears to export and import similar goods and services. This raises the possibility that other forces may help to explain trade between nations.

(8) Other matters. Having established the fact that the real wages in FOREIGN are lower than in HOME and, that after trade, both FOREIGN and HOME workers benefit, let us note the following:

(A) Since the higher real wage in HOME is productivity-driven, it is not an impediment to trading with a low-real-wage country. It is often argued that high wage countries cannot compete with low wage countries. They can if the high real wage is based on productivity differences. What is important is not the wage, but per unit costs. High real wages are consistent with low per unit costs and prices.

(B) FOREIGN can only engage in trade on the basis of low real wages. Given its lower productivity, it can export cloth only if its real wage before trade is from one third to a half as large as in HOME.

(C) By trading with a low-wage country, HOME is not exploiting that country. It is the way by which the real wage is raised in FOREIGN.

(D) Trading with a low-wage country does not harm the labor in the high-wage country since it does not alter the distribution of income in HOME. In fact, it raises the real income in HOME.

(E) It will be harmful to workers in FOREIGN for HOME to insist that it must pay its workers on a par with HOME workers (the level playing field) or that HOME will not conduct trade with FOREIGN until its workers are paid a "living wage." To insist on these policies is, as viewed by the Ricardian model, to destroy the basis for trade, the vehicle for raising the real income not only of the people in FOREIGN, but also of HOME as well.

(F) Ricardo's advice on economic development is to let the market determine which goods should be exported and imported for such a strategy will likely be based on comparative advantage. If, however, a government is pursuing an industrial policy based on winners and losers, be sure the winners are sectors in which you are likely to have a comparative advantage and don't protect what appears to be the import competing sector. In terms of our simple model, Ricardo would tell HOME, do not protect, aid, or attempt to create a textile sector and he would tell FOREIGN not to protect, aid, or attempt to create a vineyard. If you do, be certain to note where the resources are coming from.

J. Eli Heckscher and Bertil Ohlin

A major limitation of the Ricardian model is that it can't explain the source of comparative advantage, as there is only one factor that is identical in both countries. That being so, how can different labor productivities exist in the two countries? Given the restriction of the model, they can't. It is most likely that Ricardo had other uses for his clever model. For a long time this wasn't important since the policy battle was with entrenched interests that wanted to manage trade. Using Ricardo, economists could explain the gains from trade and allay the fears of those who felt threatened by cheap foreign labor. During the 20th century, as the economists' case for free trade gained adherents, they became more interested in the basis for comparative advantage and, hence, the composition of trade between countries. In addition, as noted above, it is common for many countries to have import competing sectors, a phenomenon incompatible with the Ricardian model.

Between 1919 and 1933, two Swedish economists, Eli Heckscher and Bertil Ohlin, took up the task of dealing with these two shortcomings of the Ricardian model. Ohlin was a student of Heckscher and the co-recipient (with James Meade) of the 1977 Nobel Prize in Economics for his contributions to trade theory. The model they formulated has three differences from the Smith-Ricardian model. First, it is multifactor—that is, it no longer has only one factor of production. However, it retains the assumption that the factors are identical across countries. Second, as explained below, after trade begins the countries will no longer completely specialize in the production of one good: Each will have an import competing industry. Third, the introduction of trade will alter the distribution of income, i.e., it will create winners and losers among the factors of production.

Heckscher and Ohlin (hereafter H-O) began their explanation by assuming that the factors of production are not distributed equally geographically. Some regions are rich in labor relative to land (land includes climate) and vice versa for others and the same with capital. The unequal distribution will lead to different factor prices across countries. The abundant factor in each country will have a low price relative to its price abroad while its scarce factor will command a higher price. As a consequence, goods and services that make abundant use of the plentiful factor will be cheap relative to their price abroad. Given technology and the same tastes and preferences across countries, unequal factor endowments will produce different pre-trade price ratios between the products, creating trade between countries. This leads to the conclusion that countries will tend to produce and export those goods and services which embody their abundant factor and import those which embody its scarce factor (or the abundant factor of the other countries). This type of trade is referred to as **inter-industry** trade.

There are, however, several important consequences that follow from the introduction of an additional factor of production. They must not be perfect substitutes. If they are, then we have only one factor. For expositional purposes, the subsequent discussion will be in a two-country, two-commodity world. The technology is such that both factors are needed in the production of the two goods and that technology is the same in both countries.

Because the factors are not perfect substitutes, after trade begins, the factors set free in the contracting industry will not be in the same combination as those currently employed in the expanding industry. Too much of the scarce factor and too little of the plentiful factor will be released. Thus, the additional output will be produced less efficiently and at a higher cost than at pre-trade levels of output. Moreover, to keep both factors employed, the price of the plentiful factor will rise and that of the scarce factor will fall. And this will redistribute income between the two factors. The share accruing to the plentiful factor will rise and that accruing to the scarce factor will fall. The degree to which factor prices change and, hence, income will be redistributed, will depend on the degree to which the factors are substitutes. The more substitutable, the smaller the redistribution.

The income redistribution consequence has posed a major public policy issue for the United States prompted by the fact that not only will the factor prices change, but after trade they will equalize across countries. That is, the price of the plentiful factor in one country will equal its scarce counterpart in the other and vice versa. This **factor price equalization** explains the opposition of the scarce factor to movements by countries to freer trade as well as opposing the immigration of another country's plentiful factor. In the U.S., labor is generally regarded as the scarce factor and capital as the plentiful factor. American labor unions have consistently voiced opposition to freer trade — they strongly opposed NAFTA as well as the Pacific Free Trade Area.

J.1 Is International Trade a Good Substitute for the International Movement of the Factors of Production?

In the Ricardian trade model, it was noted that the two options of free trade and the free mobility of the factor of production did not produce the same result. The world would be better off with free factor mobility. In that case, labor would move from the country where it has an absolute disadvantage in the production of both goods to where it has an absolute advantage in the production of both goods. That being the case world output would be produced in its most efficient location. One might ask the same about the H-O model. The answer is that it makes no difference. Under the conditions of the model, free trade and the free movement of the factors of production are very good substitutes. To see why, look at the H-O model in a slightly different way. What is being traded is not a good or a service, but a bundle of factors. HOME sends to FOREIGN, not an automobile, but the labor and capital needed to produce an automobile. The factors in the bundle are weighted in favor of its plentiful factor. This increases the supply of the scarce factor in FOREIGN. As a result, the decrease in HOME of its plentiful factor will drive up its price and the increase in FOREIGN's scarce factor will drive down its price. In both countries income redistribution will occur in favor of the plentiful factor just as it would if one concentrated on the movements of the products. Unlike the Ricardian model, the H-O model does not have some unexplained productivity advantage present in one country, but not the other. In fact, looking at the H-O model in terms of an exchange of a bundle of factors of production may be one of the important contributions that it makes to the discussion of public policy issues and how we think about these issues.

27

J.2. Why is Specialization Incomplete, or Why Does an Import-Competing Sector Remain?

The answer to this question makes use of the preceding discussion. After trade opens up, as a nation expands the output of its export good and contracts the output of its importing competing good, the factors of production are not released in the most efficient combination — too much of the scarce factor and too little of the abundant. Thus, while the output of the export good expands, it does so at a rate that decreases. Because of this, the cost of the export good at the margin rises. The opposite is true for the import-competing good as it contracts — its output declines but at a decreasing rate and, at the margin, its costs per unit declines. Since after trade begins, both countries will face the same price for the goods, the divergent movement in marginal costs works to make the import competing industry more competitive and this keeps it from extinction.[7]

J.3. Is Foreign Trade a Race to the Bottom for the Factors of Production?

According to many people who oppose trade, it *is* a race to the bottom. American workers, America's scarce factor, will have to accept the wages of the poorest countries we trade with. It will pauperize American labor – a race to the bottom of the income distribution. Well, foreign trade can also be looked as a "race to the top." Recall that the factor reward of the plentiful factor rises and the scarce factor falls. Also, consumers benefit. They have more goods and services with which to satisfy their needs and wants (or, in the words of Adam Smith, the sum of their enjoyments is increased) and benefit from lower prices.

J.4. How to Deal with Income Redistribution

Undoubtedly, one of the most contentious issues with respect to reducing trade barriers is income redistribution. Should people whose jobs

---

[7] In the examples above, the goods being traded are treated as finished products. Realistically, this is unlikely to be the case. About 60 percent of U.S. imports are not final goods, but intermediate goods used in the production of consumer and capital goods. The analysis still holds, but how we should think about trade may be affected.

have been eliminated or the owners of capital made redundant by lowering trade barriers be treated differently from peoples who jobs have been eliminated or whose capital is now redundant due to changes in, for example, technology? Should auto workers in Ohio, for example, whose jobs ended when the good or service they produced is now sourced in Mexico, be given job retraining at federal government expense when the workers at countless shopping malls across the country who lose their jobs and the owners of those malls whose capital is made redundant due to Amazon's retail sales revolution do not? Similarly, should workers and capital that suddenly face growing competition from imports receive protection from the government to curtail the competition? Computer-based technology is revolutionizing the entire structure of industries. Should we, like the ancient Luddites, break up the machines to save jobs?[8] Creative destruction, in the words of Joseph Schumpeter, is the essence of capitalism. This public policy issue is one that will be with us for some time. Perhaps, it is best to be guided by a simple rule. Do no harm. Do not aid others in retaining their jobs if it means that others must lose theirs.

J.5. Comparative Advantage Can Change

Comparative advantage is not a given. It changes because factor proportions change. This can happen because population growth, the source of its labor force, can change, as can the saving rate of a nation, which determines its rate of capital accumulation. In addition, technology is not constant, and this can change comparative advantage. Also, changes abroad can affect relative prices over the whole trading world, changing what these countries produce and their income distribution. It is worth noting what some of these have been.

(1) The U.S. has changed from a nation whose exports were raw materials to one whose exports are capital and consumer goods.

---

[8] The Luddites were individuals in England who, based on the technology of the time, wove cloth by using hand looms. A series of inventions made it possible to weave cloth by machines much more cheaply. The Luddites quite rightly saw the destruction of their livelihood and, in their despair, organized and attempted to destroy the machines as they were being introduced. Their efforts span the period 1811 to 1816. They were unsuccessful and the textile industry was revolutionized in Britain.

(2) The labor force growth rate has changed for several countries. Japan and China's birth rates are now below replacement rates and the Mexican birth rate has fallen noticeably. These can be explained by government policy on birth (such as the liberalization of abortions and limiting family size), the rise in real per capita income, the rise in the labor force participation rate of women, etc.

(3) Changes in the national saving rates of countries affect the rate of capital formation. These changes can also be linked to the change in birth rates and the aging of a country's population.

(4) Countries can discover new resources which can alter the basis for trade, for instance, the discovery of oil and natural gas in the Netherlands and Great Britain as well in Russia (Siberia). Advances in transportation have made possible markets for temperate fruit products grown in South America to be sold in the winter in North America.

(5) The disintegration of the Soviet Union and the opening of China to world trade have affected the post-trade relative factor prices in many countries and these have income distribution consequences for those countries.

K. Paul Krugman

The inter-industry type of trade embedded in the H-O model based on comparative advantage and relative factor endowments explains quite well a large amount of world trade. (Some 60 percent of world trade is in components and raw materials.) However, it does not explain an important amount of world trade that takes place between countries whose resource endowments, tastes and preferences, and states of development are all quite similar. For example, the trade data presented in Table 2 above show that America's top eight trading partners are nations that have factor endowments quite similar to our own. The type of trade among us is often in goods and services of a similar nature (consumer goods and services), and frequently these eight countries will both import and export similar goods and services, which is inconsistent with the type of trade predicted by the H-O model.

Why do countries with similar resource endowments find it advantageous to trade with each other? Paul Krugman, in a series of innovative papers, provided an answer which earned him the Nobel Prize in Economics in 2008. He concluded that it is due to a combination of: (1) the existence of "scale economies" in the production process and (2) a

30

market structure characterized by imperfect or monopolistic competition. This is the notion that many products, especially consumer goods and services, while similar, are distinguishable in the minds of buyers. Thus, they are imperfect substitutes for each other.

In isolation, because of similar factor endowments, per capita incomes, technology, and general tastes and preferences, countries would come to produce a similar range of goods and services. In the presence of scale economies, some of these countries would produces some of these goods and services at a lower cost than others. After trade opens up, these would be the exportable goods and the importable goods would be those in which the other countries would achieve scale economies first. This type of trade is called **intra-industry trade.** Thus, countries with similar factor endowments would both import and export similar goods and services. Factor endowments alone, then, cannot be used to predict or explain the pattern of trade. Slight differences in tastes and preferences across countries can also account for pre-trade price differences. It is an interesting fact that countries tend to export goods and services for which they have a large domestic market.

K.1 Implications of Intra-Industry Trade

(1) This type of trade should have less in the way of income redistribution than inter-industry trade. This is because as the factors of production are shifted from producing one type of good or service to producing a good substitute, they are released in about the same proportions as they are needed to expand the production of the substitute. Hence, little in the way of income redistribution is involved. Looked at from the perspective of exports and imports as bundles of factors, both bundles contain about the same proportion of factors. When imports replace domestic production, they release factors in about the same proportion needed to expand exports. Most of the gains from this type of trade come from expanding the "sum of enjoyments," or increasing the range and types of goods and services that are available to satisfy human needs and wants; they are not gains that come from using the world's resources more efficiently. It can be argued that the product differentiation on which some intra-industry trade depends is created by advertising. That is, the product differentiation is contrived. Some economists argue that this type of trade involves a waste of resources.

The data seem to suggest that intra-industry trade, especially in the case of the U.S. is diminishing — that is, U.S. trade is increasingly dominated by inter-industry trade.[9] This may, in large measure, be due to the increased U.S. dependence on imported energy. Recent technological changes have reversed this trend and the U.S. is reducing its dependence on imported petroleum.

(2) The growth of multinational companies. One of the striking features of the post-World War II era has been the growth of the multinational company. The simple H-O model posits that cloth is produced in one country and wine in the other and after trade begins each will have an import competing sector. Does it make a difference if some of the cloth firms in FOREIGN are owned by citizens of HOME and vice versa for vineyards? From the perspective of explaining the causes of comparative advantage, ownership doesn't matter as it doesn't alter relative factor endowments. This is similar for the goods and services that are the basis for intra industry trade. Foreign ownership may, however, make the exploitation of the factor possible and it will, as seen below, affect a nation's balance of payments.

(3) The dynamic gains from trade. The gains from trade thus far identified are what are called "static gains" since they arise from the reallocation of a given amount of resources. Trade also generates what are called "dynamic gains" and these may be the most important effect on an economy. Dynamic gains include such growth enhancing things as capital equipment, new and advanced technology embodied in this capital, technical know-how skills, managerial talents, entrepreneurial ability, etc. To the extent such developments increase the growth rate of a country they will generate a higher level of saving contributing to a higher level of investment and an increase in per capital income.

(4) Measuring the gains from trade. It is not easy to measure the gains from trade as history does not allow us to see how the world would have been with or without freer trade. Moreover, it is hard to measure the satisfaction to individuals that accrue from having more and a greater variety of goods and services to consume. Nevertheless, the topic is of interest and several substitute measures have been formulated. A popular measure is quantitative: How many units of imports does a nation receive for each unit of exports that it gives up. This is called the **net barter terms**

---

[9] See Paul Krugman's Nobel Lecture, "The Increasing Returns Revolution in Trade and Geography," *American Economic Review,* June 2009: 561-571.

of trade. If the number rises, the nation is supposedly better off. This index is compiled by dividing the price of exports by the price of imports.

A difficulty with this measure is that it does not measure how many imports a nation gets for the factors of production (labor and capital) that must be given up for the imports. In fact, should the factors become more productive, it can give the wrong answer. Alternative measures have been developed to remedy these shortcomings, but they also suffer measurement problems. And, as shown below, the terms of trade are sensitive to a nation's net international capital position and have nothing to do with gains or losses for a country.

L. Summary

The discussion in this section has looked at two alternative approaches to international trade formulated in terms of what is popularly termed "industrial policy." The older of the two, Mercantilism, envisioned an important role for the government in determining what is produced, how it is produced, where it is produced, and to whom the output is given. Government policy was substantially influenced by those who would benefit from it. Prominent among the devices used by government to influence production were export subsidies, grants of monopoly to produce certain goods and services or to exploit a given product or geographic area, use of guilds and other devices to affect employment and wages, the use of tariffs and quotas to shelter and encourage the production of import substitutes, etc. All this was done with little attention paid to whether capital and labor were allocated to efficient production, what were the economic costs of this misallocation, and the absence of concern for the interests of consumers. Public policies pertaining to foreign trade focused on exports and the achievement of the largest export surplus or favorable balance of trade possible. That trade might be mutually beneficial was dismissed. The wealth of a nation depended on production and the exportation of what was produced. The emphasis was on the nation state and, thus, was nationalistic.

The alternative is based on a far different and much more limited role for government in formulating an industrial policy. In so far as trade is concerned the alternative viewed international exchange, like domestic exchange, as mutually beneficial — if that were not true, exchange would not take place. Freeing trade from tariffs and quotas expanded the amount and variety of goods and services, or the "sum of enjoyments" available to

33

consumers. It pointed out the impossibility that all nations could simultaneously achieve a favorable trade balance and it developed a theory of the role of money and prices in making a favorable trade balance an impossible steady state position for an individual nation. It emphasized that the wealth of a nation depended on how efficiently its capital and labor were employed, and that this was inconsistent with propping-up import substitute industries with tariffs and quotas. It emphasized that individuals should be free to choose their occupations and how they allocated their savings to investments of their choice. The emphasis of this challenge to Mercantilism was both appealing to economists as well as multinational in its focus. It also had indirect benefits. For example, since its focus was international it encouraged the resolution of potential world conflicts by peaceful means. International institutions were set up to moderate conflicts and encourage the free movement of goods and services.

II. Barriers to Trade

The human mind is very inventive when it comes to impeding trade. It would vastly expand this book if all the impediments were explored. The following highlights just a few of the more popular ones and returns us to another discussion of Mercantilism for the origin of many and their use can be traced to the time that doctrine dominated public policy.

A. Tariffs

Perhaps the oldest barrier to trade is the tariff or tax on imported goods. The word *tariff* is also used to mean the "schedule of taxes." It was not originally used as a barrier to trade but as the major revenue source for governments, often because it is easy to collect. The ancient Romans used this tax and one on land to finance their expenditures. As noted above, it was also the dominant tax used by the U.S. federal government until the Civil War.[10] We shall see, however, that despite the wishes of the Founding Fathers, laying taxes on imports will lay an equal tax on exports.

This tax can be express as either a **percent of value (ad valorem)**, or as a **specific amount** per unit of the good, or as a combination of the two. It is not clear which type of tariff is easier to administer, but its degree of protection can be quite different in the face of changes in the price of imports. The protection afforded by ad valorem tariffs is insensitive to such changes while that of a specific tariff is inverse to a change in import prices.

It has long been a question about who pays this tax. Since this is a tax on imports it is like a sales tax. Such a tax is paid by the buyer as it is added to the price of the good or service purchased. However, this tax can under certain circumstances be shifted backward; that is, the incidence of the tax is shifted in part to the seller. This can occur if the buyer accounts for a large part of the purchases. It can happen in this way. The tax raises the price of the good to the buyer. The **quantity demanded** by the buyer

---

[10] The U.S. Constitution forbids the laying of taxes on exports: see Article I Section 9, clause 5: "Congress shall not levy a tax or duty on any good or service exported from any U.S. state."

declines. If this decline is large, the **demand** for the good in the world market can fall and with it the before tax price. The tax is now computed on this reduced world price, and the price paid by the buyer will be less than it would have been if the pre-tax price hadn't fallen. Thus, part of the tax will be shifted back to the sellers in the form of a decline in the after-tax price they receive.

Like all taxes, the tariff has certain costs to the public. The rise in price will attract resources to expand domestic output. This additional output represents an inefficient use of the nation's resources and is wasteful. Second, buyers will have to pay a higher price so they reduce the quantity consumed. On each of these units they will suffer a loss of satisfaction (called consumer surplus). These two losses are the cost or **dead-weight** burden (meaning a burden for which no offsetting gain occurs) to the society for imposing the tariff in excess of what they paid for the good or service before the tax was imposed.

A.1. The Effective Rate of Protection of a Tariff

The increasing globalization of supply chains complicates measuring the degree of protection afforded by a tariff. The analysis thus far is of a tax imposed on a good that is wholly made within the country of origin. That is, the country imposing the tariff does not produce a substitute in whole or part. Often this is not the case: some 60 percent of U.S. imports are parts and components. Consider the case where the country imposing the tariff may produce some part of product or that product has some domestic value added. With the growth of global supply chains this is likely to be increasingly true. Does this alter how to look at the protective nature of a tariff? The answer is yes. Take the case of a car whose international price is $20,000. A country does not produce a complete car, but assembles $16,000 in parts it imports. Thus, its domestic value added is $4,000. It now considers expanding its own auto industry to include assembly and imposes a 25 percent tax on imported cars. As a result, the cars it produces can now sell for $25,000 and the domestic value added can expand from $4,000 to $9,000 or $5,000. Based on its original value added of $4,000, the increase afforded by a 25 percent tariff is now more than 125 percent of its original value added. Thus, the **effective rate of protection** on its value added, 125 percent, is five times larger than the original nominal tariff of 25 percent on the completed motor vehicle.

36

Alternatively, the country may now want to increase its auto parts industry so it imposes a 25 percent tariff on imported parts. The imported parts increase to $20,000 and, without an increase in the tariff on completed vehicles, the maximum value added in that sector drops to zero.

While this choice is highly unlikely, it does demonstrate the point that the higher the tariff on the low end of the production chain, the less protective is the existing tariff on the high end of the chain.

Considerations such as this influence the type of international tariff-reduction negotiations that nations conduct. Underdeveloped countries who wish to develop by expanding sales in developed countries will urge these countries to lower their tariff on finished goods whereas developed countries will want to keep the tariffs on completed goods high and reduce those on imported components.

A.2. Arguments for a Tariff

There have been several arguments put forth by reasonable people to justify a **protective** tariff. Two in particular stand out.

(1) **Infant industry**. This argument holds that in certain industries the production process is likely to yield large economies of scale. For a nation to benefit from these economies, it must protect its own market so that the industry can expand and realize the scale economies and thus become a viable domestic industry serving the domestic market at the expense of imports or even become an exporter. Alexander Hamilton was an early advocate of this view to encourage American manufacturing and economic development in general.

There are a number of arguments against this rationale for a tariff. It is hard to identify a promising infant; infants seldom grow up; if you want to encourage an infant, do so with a subsidy it is more transparent; and this argument turns Smith's argument for free trade on its head. (Recall that Smith argued that trade would expand the market, allowing any external economies of scale to be realized.)

(2) **National security**. This argument is that a nation needs certain types of economic activity for its national security and this justifies a tariff to keep domestic firms that supply this type of activity in existence. This argument arose recently in a number of cases: it became known that the rocket engines used by the U.S. to supply the space station are purchased from Russia; the U.S. steel and automobile industries are needed for defense and both are threatened by China; and a number of drugs

important for the health of Americans are sourced in both China and India, etc.

The argument for free trade does not mean that some activities cannot be protected for purposes of national security. Adam Smith justified the Navigation Acts, which restricted the trade of Great Britain to British-owned and -manned ships as necessary to the national security of an island country. Many in Britain opposed the slave trade, and in more recent times, the drug traffic has been subject to control. Care, however, must be applied to selecting these activities so that they are not extended to any activity that does not want to compete with foreign firms. Moreover, there are others means of protection that are more transparent so that the citizen knows exactly what protection costs. This alternative is called a subsidy whose recipient and amount can be a line item in the government budget.

A.3. Why Not Just Abolish All Tariffs?

The discussion above has identified a number of undesirable effects from tariffs centering on the inefficient use of resources and the curtailment of the goods and services available to consumers. This being the case why don't nations just abolish tariffs unilaterally rather than negotiate tariff reductions? Possible reasons against unilateral abolishment would be: (1) they may need them for government revenue especially if they can shift their incidence backward; (2) it may be difficult to do so since they may benefit a small number of people who are highly organized relative to those who have to bear their burdens; (3) they protect industries considered vital for national security.

B. Quotas

While a tariff is a monetary means to restrict trade, a quota does so by imposing an absolute limit on the amount of goods that can be imported into a country. This is a physical limit such as 10,000 pounds of sugar, 500 tons of copper, 400,000 automobiles, etc. The effect of the quota, like a tariff, is to raise prices of imports so that a certain share of the home market is reserved for domestic producers. Over time, as demand grows, a quota is more restrictive than a tariff in protecting markets. Like a tariff, a quota can be a source of revenue to a government. It depends on how the government imposes the quota. It can auction it to the public in which case the value of the quota accrues to it. It can give the quota to the foreign

38

government and let it sell the rights and that government receives the revenue, or the quota can simply be given directly to the exporter and they receive the value of the quota. Regardless of what method is used, the quota involves the same dead-weight losses as a tariff.

C. Export Subsidies[11]

A number of countries subsidize exports, or it is claimed that they do. In the U.S., the principal type of subsidy is by affecting the flow of credit to export industries. That is, the U.S. government through the Export Import (EXIM) Bank will guarantee the loans that U.S. banks make to finance foreign purchases of U.S. goods. This reduces the risk of the sale and, as a consequence, the cost of credit for foreign companies who are considering the purchase of those goods. The largest user of the EXIM Bank has been the Boeing Company.

Subsidizing exports reduces their price in a very real way. They therefore have a "terms of trade" effect, they keep resources employed inefficiently, and they are a burden to taxpayers. While it may sound paradoxical, export subsidies designed to help domestic firms penetrate foreign markets actually subsidize the indigenous export firms in those same foreign markets. The subsidies given to domestic exporters by a government increases the imports of foreign countries. To buy the now cheaper imports, they supply additional domestic money to the foreign exchange market. This causes their exchange rate to depreciate, making their goods cheaper to the country doing the subsidizing and increasing the quantity of imports from those countries. By how much will these induced imports increase? In the absence of a capital movement, the amount will be exactly equal to the additional exports made possible by its subsidies. Will the foreign export firms realize their good fortune? Unlikely. If they do, they will be drowned out by the complaints of import-competing firms who must now face the cheaper competition made possible by the subsidized prices of their imports. Recall a conclusion noted at the beginning of this book: In the absence of a net international capital flow, goods and services exported must equal in value those imported. Thus, public policy choices that increase exports will also increase imports and have income redistribution consequences.

---

[11] One can think of export subsidies as negative taxes. Thus, the arguments applying to taxes, apply also to negative taxes.

D. Domestic Content Requirements

The purpose of domestic content requirements is to increase or preserve employment in a given industry. The renegotiated NAFTA treaty increased the North American domestic content or value added before the items could pass from Mexico to the United States duty-free. This shifts production from Mexico to the U.S. or forestalls U.S. firms from moving to Mexico. A variation on the domestic content requirement is that a certain proportion of production must be done in a plant that pays a certain wage. Domestic-content requirements are also found in the entertainment industry. European filmmakers have long felt threatened by films made in Hollywood. To protect their own industry, they have gotten their governments to specify that so many hours of prime-time television must be from local film studios.

E. Other Measures

Many other measures exist that interfere with trade, some of which are imposed to accomplish such worthy goals as the health and safety of a nation. An example is specifying that a good may not be sold if it contains artificial steroids or growth hormones. Rather somewhat less worthy is the requirement that domestically produced products must be given preference in government purchases over those from abroad even if the latter are cheaper ("Buy American"). Petty means like lengthening customs procedures, requiring additional trade documents, classification disputes for tariffs, additional packaging, labelling or product standards, and so forth are employed to make foreign trade more costly and, thus, reduce it.

F. Dumping

A very popular reason why countries impede trade is that they accuse other countries of **dumping.** Even the word sounds evil. In popular terms, no one likes to be dumped on. American political leaders, voicing the opinions of business firms in their districts, especially if they are steel producers, constantly accuse China of building steel capacity far in excess of world needs for it. To contain their inventories of steel, Chinese firms, it is argued, sell it on the world market at below the cost to produce it —

the legal essence of dumping. This works a hardship on American producers and they seek relief by asking the U.S. Commerce Department to impose anti-dumping duties on Chinese firms in order to "level the playing field."

While dumping is defined in law to be selling at below cost, it is never quite certain whose cost is being used to prove the case — probably the highest cost producer in the country. Economists look at dumping in a different way as a method for increasing a seller's profits. They note that the aggregate demand for a good in a given market consists of summing many individual demands which are not equally urgent. Some buyers have alternatives for the good or service, others do not. Although all will pay the same price, it will be to the seller's advantage if that were not the case. Rather, it will be to the seller's advantage if the buyers can be grouped by the urgency with which they want the good. Those most urgent will pay a higher price than those less urgent. Anyone looking at this market will see different prices charged to different customers even though the price differences cannot be cost justified. In fact, it may cost the seller the same to sell to each customer. Notice that those charged a higher price are not subsidizing the lower price given other customers. It is more profitable to sell this way than for the seller to give all buyers the same price.

International trade provides the conditions for this type of price discrimination. Often domestic buyers have fewer alternative sellers for a host of products than do buyers in foreign countries, and domestic sellers have ways to separate domestic from foreign markets (such as tariffs and quotas). One problem that may arise in this situation is that the buyers who get the lower price may attempt to become sellers and, by resale, attempt to take customers away from the primary seller.

Dumping raises the question of who benefits from this practice. Clearly, the sellers can increase their profits and those customers who buy at a lower price than they would have had to pay if the practice was not illegal. From this perspective, countervailing duties are anti-competitive.

III. The International Balance of Payments

The international balance of payments, shown in Table 5, records the transactions of individuals, businesses, and governments of one country with similar parties in the rest of the world. It makes no difference in what monetary unit these transactions are concluded. A majority are most likely made in U.S. dollars as it has become an international monetary unit.

The balance of payments (BoP) is divided into two parts: the **current account,** which measures flows of goods and services, and the **capital and financial account,** which measures changes in a country's net international assets position or changes in stocks. The BoP obeys the conventional rules devised by accountants in the construction of the two accounts found in businesses: the profit and loss (or income) statement and the balance sheet. The current account corresponds to the former while the financial account the latter. In BoP accounting, the country is treated as a business unit.

The two parts of the BoP are interconnected as they are constructed using what is known as **double entry** bookkeeping. This means that every **initiating or autonomous** transaction gives rise to a second **induced** or **accommodating** transaction that explains how it is financed. Thus, most, but not all, of the transactions, involve both parts of the BoP. The BoP uses the same terminology as would be found in the two business statements. The sale of goods and services by a business would be entered on its books as a **credit** (and given a plus sign). Similarly, the word *credit* is used to record the export or sale abroad of goods and services and the word **debit** (given a negative sign) is used by a business when it purchases goods and services and, in the BoP accounting, for imports or the purchases of goods and services from abroad. A current account surplus would be expressed with a plus sign, while a deficit would be recorded with a minus sign.

Since the financial account corresponds to the balance sheet used by a business, the word *credit* applies to all increases in foreign claims on the U.S. (or on U.S. liabilities to foreigners) and *debit* to all increases in U.S. ownership of foreign assets. Thus, should a U.S. business firm buy a foreign firm, the initial transaction would be recorded as a debit on the financial account. This use of the word *debit* is consistent with its use in the current account. In the current account, the debit indicates that Americans are buying foreign goods and services. In the financial account, it means that Americans are buying foreign assets (the shares of foreign firms). Similarly, should the Japanese government buy U.S. Treasury bonds, the transaction would be recorded as a credit in the financial account just as a business would record a loan received from a bank as an increase in its liabilities on its balance sheet. From this discussion, it can be seen that the financial account records transactions by both private individuals and governments. These two types of transactions are presented separately. Some individuals focus heavily on the international financial transactions of governments and attempt to link them to movements in the exchange rate of the dollar.

Table 5
International Balance of Payments

Current Account	Capital and Financial Account
A. Goods	*A. Capital Account Transactions*
Exports (+)	*B. U.S. Owned Assets Abroad*
Imports (-)	U.S. Official Assets
B. Services	Other U.S. Government Assets
Net Military Transactions	Private Assets
Net Travel & Transport	*C. Foreign Owned Assets in U.S.*
Net Other Services	Foreign Official Assets
C. Primary Income	Other (Private) Assets
Receipts (+)	*D. Errors and Omissions*
Payments (-)	
D. Secondary Income	
Receipts (+)	
Payments (-)	
A + B = Balance on Goods and Services	B + C = Balance on Financial Account
C + D = Income Balance	
A + B + C + D = Current Account Balance	A + B + C + D = Balance on Capital and Financial Account

Notes: Primary income is wages, interest, and dividends. Secondary income is unilateral transfers such as remittances and gifts. "Net" items can be either positive or negative. All items on the capital and financial account side are net.

There are some transactions that do not use both parts of the BoP. Take, as an example, the case where the U.S. provides aid to a foreign country hit by a natural disaster – hurricane, earthquake, flood, epidemic, etc. The value of the aid would be recorded as an export of goods and services (credit). The offsetting debit would be recorded as a **unilateral transfer** (a transfer for which no quid pro quo is expected — both are in the current account).

As the balance of payments is constructed by accountants, the current account balance is exactly offset by the balance on the financial account — thus the two parts of the balance of payments always sum to zero. There is neither a surplus nor deficit.[12] It is very important to note that BoP balance in the accounting sense does not necessarily mean that the balance of payments is in equilibrium.

If the balance of payments is always in balance, what do people mean when they talk about a balance of payments deficit or surplus? They usually have one of four measures in mind: (1) the **balance on goods** (sometimes referred to as the balance of trade or visibles); (2) the **balance on goods and services** (sometimes this is also referred to as the balance of trade); (3) the **balance on current account**; and (4) a measure of government intervention in the foreign exchange market that is recorded in the financial account as the sum of **U.S. Official Reserve** assets and **Foreign Official** assets. This is called the **Official Settlements Balance** or **Official Reserve Transactions Balance.** Despite claims that these are measures of disequilibrium (both deficit and surplus and + or -), they are not. They are perfectly consistent with equilibrium conditions. Thus, the nearly continuous current account deficits for the U.S. since 1970 shown on Figure 1 are consistent with equilibrium.

There is one very interesting aspect of looking at the balances in both sides of the BoP document: They tell us about the nature and composition of international capital flows. If a country is the recipient of a **net** inflow of capital from abroad it will have a debit balance on its current account and a credit balance on its financial account. **What is involved here is a net _outflow_ of financial paper and a net _inflow_ of goods and services.** And this is the essence of the international flow of capital. It is not a net

---

[12] Since the balance of payments data are gathered by sampling, this is not literally the case and when the published statements are presented, they are accompanied by a column entitled "statistical discrepancy" which reflects that fact. It is thought that the financial transactions are likely to be the major source of errors.

inflow of brick and mortar with which to build a factory, but of goods and services in general.[13]

The fact that the two sides of the balance of payments account offset each other, tells us little if anything about the causality involved. Does the existence of the net inflow of capital cause the current account deficit or is it the other way around? Was the net capital inflow needed to finance the excess of goods and services purchased? Before this topic can be discussed, it will be necessary to discuss the foreign exchange market.

---

[13] And herein lies the potential loss from international capital movements. For example, a large amount of Japanese capital came to the U.S. when the exchange rate was about 400 yen to the dollar. Were this capital to be repatriated by the Japanese, they could get about 100 yen or so per every dollar. This would result in a large wealth transfer to the U.S.

IV. The Foreign Exchange Market

The foreign exchange rate is the price of one country's currency in terms of another's, and like other prices, it is determined by supply and demand. It is an **endogenous** variable, one that is determined by the interaction of all other variables in the system as opposed to a variable that is given or said to be **exogenous** (see Appendix B).

The foreign exchange rate can be expressed in two ways: (1) how many units of a foreign currency do I get for each unit of my country's currency (e.g., 8 Argentine pesos for each U.S. dollar) or (2) how much does each unit of foreign currency cost in terms of U.S. dollars (each Argentine peso costs about 12 U.S. cents). These two measures are reciprocals. Furthermore, this price is special in the sense that it is the means by which the prices of the world's goods and services are converted into those of the focus country.

A. The Nominal and the Real Exchange Rate

The exchange rates published in the financial section of newspapers or on the internet are nominal exchange rates. That is, they are not adjusted for the differences in national price levels. And this can cause misunderstandings about what each currency can buy abroad and how to interpret changes in those rates over time. Suppose, for example, that $1 exchanges for 20 Mexican pesos. Does this mean that the purchasing power of the dollars is twenty times that of the peso? It may, but suppose the price level in Mexico is twenty times that in the U.S. In this case, the dollar buys the same market basket as would 20 pesos. Thus, the nominal rate is the same as the real rate. Take as an alternative a case in which $1 again exchanges for 20 pesos and both buy the same market basket of goods and services. Now, let the price level in the Mexico double and the market value of the peso rise to $1 = 40 pesos. Has the real value of the dollar doubled? At 40 pesos to the dollar, both still buy the same market basket.

This distinction is vitally important. Various shocks can affect a nations' economy that require the exchange rate to change and it is the **real rate** that must do the adjusting. Thus, all changes in nominal rates must not be interpreted as equivalent changes in real rates. And the exchange rate must not be interpreted as an **exogenous** variable or one given to the system, a mistake frequently made by media pundits. It is common for them to say such things as: the depreciation of the dollar should help U.S. growth or vice versa for an appreciation. Unless it is known what has caused the change in the exchanges rate, such statements are likely to be in error.

Changes in the exchange rate, and the factors that generate those changes, are best described in terms of the underlying supply and demand curves in the foreign exchange market, as shown in Figure 2. The supply curve is directly derived from a nation's international spending (or demand) for the goods, services, and assets of the reset of the world, while the demand curve similarly emerges from spending (or demand) by the rest of the world for its goods, services and assets. Let's see why this is likely to be the case. The vertical axis measures the number of units of FOREIGN's money that can be exchanges for one unit of HOME's money. Given the price level in both countries, the vertical axis measures the real exchange rate (or the net barter terms of trade, or e). As the real exchange rises (or appreciates), it will cost FOREIGN more to buy the goods and services of HOME and they will shift their purchases to their own substitutes. As a result, the quantity of HOME's money demanded by FOREIGN should be expected to decline and the demand curve will slope downward and to the right. As the real exchange rate rises, the quantity of FOREIGN's goods and services purchased or demanded by HOME should, under usual circumstances, be expected to rise. The amount of HOME'S money supplied to the foreign exchange market to make these purchases will depend on how much the demand for goods and services rises relative to the decline in the real price of them — but it is generally expected to be upward sloping (for a more extensive discussion of this issue, see Appendix C).

Three things to note about this market: (1) both the vertical and horizontal axis measure real quantities — the former, the real exchange rate, or the net barter terms of trade and the latter, the real quantities of goods and services; (2) it contains the demand and supply of money to purchase and sell items that enter both the GDP and non-GDP accounts, e.g., used cars and financial assets; (3) and does not involve the unilateral transfer items in the balance of payments.

Figure 2
Foreign Exchange Market

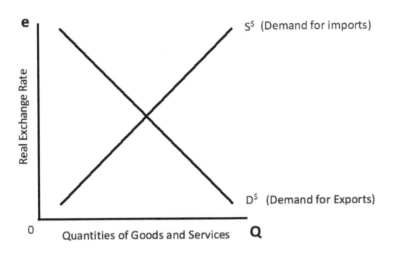

Like the supply and demand curves used to explain the price of a single good, it is important to know what determines the **elasticity** (or slope) of these curves and what causes them to **shift.**

Elasticity. The elasticity (or slope of the supply and demand curves) depends on the degree to which the goods and services produced abroad are substitutes for those produced at home. The greater the substitutability, the more elastic (or flatter) is the curve because small changes in price will lead to large changes in the quantity demanded. Thus, if inter-industry trade dominates, the curves are likely to be more elastic than if trade is dominated by intra-industry trade.

Financial assets. Does the demand for financial assets also depend on the real exchange rate? It seems as though it might. After all, the more foreign currency one gets per dollar, the greater will be the number of financial securities one can buy. As appealing as it sounds, it may not be true. Financial assets flow from one country to another based on their respective rates of return. The rate of return, or yield, is calculated by dividing the divided or interest payment by the price of the security. Since both are changed in the same way by changes in the exchange rate, their yield in unaffected. Thus, changes in the exchange rate will not affect their demand or supply and have no effect on either curve's **elasticity.** The **net flow**, as shown in Figure 3, will be treated as an add on to the existing demand or supply schedule for goods and services depending on whether it is positive or negative.

Figure 3
Foreign Exchange Market with Net Capital Inflow

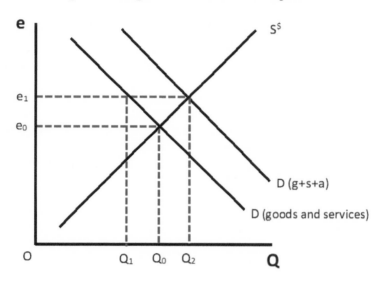

O Q1 = Exports
O Q2 = Imports
O Q2 – O Q1 = Trade deficit or net export of financial assets

Shiftability. What types of changes or shocks will cause the curves to shift? Among them will be changes in *(1)* real income, *(2)* relative prices of goods and services, *(3)* tastes and preferences, *(4)* impending devaluations or revaluations, political and/or economic instability and *(5)* expected real rate of return on assets (FOREIGN vs. HOME). Number (5) requires additional clarification. Changes in national real rates of return can affect the international flow of capital. How large this effect will be depends on the degree to which the financial assets of the world are substitutes for each other. We speak of **integrated international capital markets**: this means that the financial assets of the various countries are good substitutes for each other. If relative national real interest rates change, the real exchange rate will change since it will induce a capital flow in pursuit of the changed yields. Before discussing the linkage between the balance of payments and the foreign exchange rate, it will be necessary to discuss the two types of exchange rate regimes.

B. Fixed vs. Flexible Exchange Rate Regimes[14]

In an important sense, the distinction between fixed and flexible exchange rate regimes is largely a non-discussion. Both fixed and flexible exchange rates are actually flexible. When an economic shock requires the exchange rate to change, it is the real rate that must change regardless of what nominal exchange rate regime is in place. The means by which the real rate changes, however, is the distinguishing feature of the regime. In a flexible rate regime, the nominal rate is market determined. If, for example, the real rate must change, this will be brought about by a shift in either the supply or demand curve in the foreign exchange market. Given the price level in the relevant countries, the change in the nominal rate will bring about an immediate change in the real rate. In the fixed exchange rate regime the adjustment is more complex. The shift in either the supply or demand curve will behave exactly as noted above. However, as the nominal exchange rate is fixed, these shifts will create either an excess demand or supply of money in the foreign exchange market at the prevailing nominal rate. And this will lead to money flowing from one country to others. The price level in the country losing money will fall and the price level in the countries gaining money will rise. This is David Hume's price specie flow mechanism at work and it is this change in national price levels that will change the real exchange rate and restore an equilibrium in which the export and import of goods and services are again equal. The more substitutable are the goods and services between countries, the less will the national prices levels have to change. (Recall that in the Ricardian and H-O inter-industry trade, the goods are perfect substitutes, while in the Krugman intra-industry trade they are not. Thus adjustment should be quicker in the former.)

The following four examples will help understand the connection between the balance of payments and the foreign exchange market. They will be repeated in a slightly altered form when we look at them in the

---

[14] For a more extensive discussion of the two regimes see Appendix D.

context of the macroeconomic model that will complete our discussion. For ease of exposition, these examples will assume a flexible exchange rate regime. They will all begin with a balanced current account (meaning no net movement in financial assets).

(1) HOME's citizens shift from buying their own goods and services to FOREIGN's substitutes (due perhaps to a change in tastes and preferences or relative price changes). As shown in Figure 4, this results in an increase in the supply of HOME's money in the foreign exchange market and a depreciation of its currency (move from A to B). The depreciation will generate an increase in the quantity of exports demanded. In the new equilibrium, the real value of HOME's money will be lower, both imports and exports will have increased and the volume of trade will be greater (move from Q0 to Q1). This simple example establishes a truth of great importance: Goods and services (exports) pay for goods and services (imports). Let us not pass by without speculating what writers in the financial press might be tempted to make of the depreciation of HOME's money. Undoubtedly, they would express the opinion that it bodes well for further income growth and additional employment growth in HOME. Heed, however, the warning given early in the book. In drawing conclusions about what is likely to happen from a change in the international value of a country's money, do not treat the change as an exogenous variable. Inquire as to what caused it to change. In the case above, depreciation has little to tell us about the future course of economic growth and employment since the balance of trade remains unchanged. When this example is viewed from the perspective of the other countries, their exports actually increase as their money **appreciates!** What would their financial press make of this development?

(2) Differential rates of national income growth. Suppose each country spends the same proportion of any increase in real per capita income on imported goods and services and, for some reason, one country begins to grow at a faster rate. This will not produce an international trade deficit, as the faster-growing country will supply a larger amount of its money to the foreign exchange market than that demanded by the now slower-growing country. As a result, the exchange rate of the faster growing country will depreciate, stimulating an increase in its exports and a decline in imports, both of which will restore balanced trade.

51

Figure 4
Change in Preferences

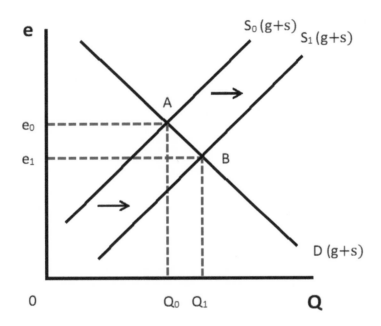

(3) Imposition of trade impediments. What would happen in this simple world if one or the other country imposed an impediment to trade such as a tariff or quota? The impediment would cause the imposing country to switch from buying foreign goods to domestic substitutes. As shown in Figure 5, this would lead to a decline in the supply of its money in the foreign exchange market causing it to **appreciate**.

This would reduce the quantity of its exports demanded by foreigners. How much would they decline? **By the same dollar amount as the tariffs or quotas depressed imports**. Let us not pass over the previous sentence lightly. **It tells us that a tax on imports is an equivalent tax on exports**. In 2020, the U.S. imposed a tariff on a variety of Chinese imports, most notably steel. Almost immediately it severely affected the export of

American farm products to China.[15] Because of this it is difficult to say what its overall effect on employment will be. It will increase in the newly protected sector and decrease in the export sector. The political leadership of the country will tout the expansion in that sector but pass over the employment lost in the export sector. The moral of the story is that when politicians impose trade impediments and tout their beneficial effects on employment, **they neglect the accompanying change in the exchange rate that has the potential to undo their great plan or reveal its emptiness.** The real ultimate effect of their scheme is to reduce the volume of trade and realign the employment of labor and capital from more to less efficient production.

Figure 5
Imposition of a Trade Barrier

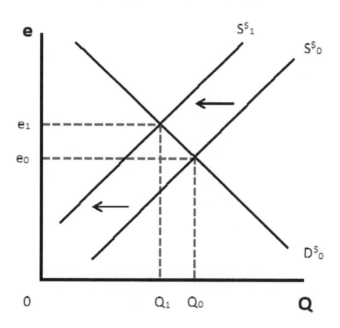

---

[15] Recall that the U.S. Constitution forbids the levying of taxes on exports. The U.S.–Chinese experience is a perfect example of a tax being levied on imports, which produces the same effect on exports as if it had been levied directly on them. What would our constitutional scholars say about this?

Figure 6
Net Purchase of HOME's Financial Assets

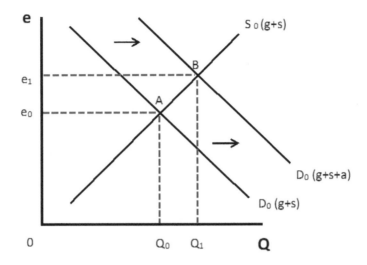

(4) Individuals, financial institutions, and governments abroad buy net HOME's financial assets. Of the cases considered in this section, this is the most complex and the least understood. The first thing to notice is that the net purchase of financial assets will show up in the exchange market, as shown in Figure 6, as a shift to the right of the demand for HOME's money. Notice it is the gap between total demand and the demand for goods and services that widens. It does so because the parties abroad must buy HOME's money before they can buy HOME's financial assets. The result is that HOME's money appreciates inducing FOREIGN to buy fewer of HOME's exports and HOME to buy more of FOREIGN's exports. The net result is that HOME now has a current account (trade) deficit equal in amount to that which FOREIGN spent net on HOME's financial assets. On the balance of payments the **initiating entry**, the purchase of financial assets, could appear in one of two places. If this is a private purchase, it will appear as **other foreign assets** (credit or a + sign); if purchased by government, it will be recorded as **foreign official assets** (also a credit and + sign). This example is full of useful information, but note first: The net inflow of capital (as well as an increase in the net inflow of imports of goods and services) is associated with an **appreciation** of

54

HOME's money (we move from point A to B). This fact will be important later in this narrative.

Table 6
Capital Flows to and from the U.S by Source (billion dollars)

	United States			Foreign		
Year	Public	Private	Total	Public	Private	Total
1970	-0.9	10.2	9.3	7.8	-0.6	7.2
1980	13.3	73.7	87.0	16.6	45.4	52.0
1990	-0.2	81.4	81.2	33.9	105.4	139.3
2000	1.2	559.3	560.5	42.8	995.5	1038.3
2005	-19.6	566.3	546.7	259.3	988.1	1247.4
2010	-5.7	945.2	939.5	398.2	918.1	1316.3
2015	-6.3	208.6	202.2	213.1	289.0	501.1
2018	5.0	305.8	310.8	315.7	419.9	735.6

Source: Bureau of Economic Analysis, U.S. Dept. of Commerce.
Note: Public capital for the U.S. is the sum of U.S. official reserve assets and other U.S. government assets. For foreign countries, public capital consists of those assets classified as foreign official while private capital are assets classified as other foreign.

Second, the net inflow of capital from abroad produces a **current account** deficit in HOME's BoP. Does this mean that the BoP is in disequilibrium? No! The inflow of private capital and the resultant current account deficit are a part of normal business transactions — the desire to maximize profits by foreigners. One cannot infer from the Current Account balance alone anything about the state of equilibrium of the balance of payments. A deficit or surplus in the current account is compatible with the normal operation of the international economy. Thus, the near run of continuous deficits in the U.S. current account since 1970 need not be something to distress policymakers. In one sense it should make the U.S. proud that we are regarded internationally as a sound place in which the world can put its savings. Alternatively, the net inflow may be the result of purchases by foreign governments. The data in Table 6 are designed to answer that question and reveal other major trends. For the United States, private capital outflow dominates as does the inflow from foreign countries. Given the similar magnitude of both flows, it would appear that while Americans find good investment opportunities abroad, foreigners find those opportunities here. However, there has been a substantial growth in capital inflow from official sources (treasuries and central banks).

Third, it is important to note the direction of **causality**. The **initiating** transaction runs from the financial account through changes in the exchange rate to the current account not the other way around.

Fourth, the relative movement in the exchange rate is of great importance. In the new equilibrium (point B), the rate for the capital importing country (which will have a current account deficit) will appreciate and be above the rate (Point A) that would prevail without the import of capital while the opposite occurs in the lending country. Its exchange rate will depreciate and lie below the rate that prevailed before the export of its capital. Many observers will look at these developments and conclude that the trade deficit resulted from **currency manipulation.** That is, the currency whose price fell did so because the government in question forced the depreciation to fulfill income growth and/or employment goals or goals linked to world domination in various industries. The current villain in the piece is China. But notice the change in the real exchange rate is an integral part of the process by which capital moves from one country to another. How much the real exchange rate will change, depends on the degree to which the goods and services of the two countries are substitutable: the more substitutable, the smaller the change.

Fifth, is it possible for causality to run in the opposite direction from the current account to the financial account? There are several arguments put forth that it does. One is popular with President Trump. Its supporters advance a novel argument and it forms one of the pillars for their position that the U.S. gets a bad deal when it comes to trade. The measure of the bad deal is the current account deficit. Not only that, but the deficit provides the financial wherewithal for foreigners to buy American assets and gain a foothold in our markets and access trade secrets by the U.S. firms in which they acquire a financial holding. Current trade practices are, thus, a win-win situation for foreigners. They don't buy our goods and the deficit provides them with our money to buy our business firms. From the information above you can see that this argument is spurious. A trade deficit cannot be produced by any device that impedes trade. The exchange rate would adjust immediately to restore balance between exports and imports, resulting in a decline in the amount of trade between nations.

Thus, this type of analysis is false. Causality based on this argument cannot run from the current account to the financial account.

Another is to be found in the report of the bipartisan Trade Deficit Review Commission established by Congress in 1998 to look into the causes and consequences of the U.S. trade deficit and to make recommendations for action.[16] In November 2000, the report of this group was published. It contains an interesting observation: "Financing a $450-billion annual trade deficit means that the United States has to attract an equally large amount of new foreign capital, net of new U.S. overseas investment." In would seem that the commission viewed causality running from the current to the financial account. No reason was given why in a flexible exchange regime such an annual trade deficit would exist.

A third possibility makes use of the fact that a large amount of international trade is conducted on the basis of credit. Thus, the flow of goods and services abroad gives rise to the flow of credit. What is neglected by this argument is that the outflow of credit both decreases the amount in the lending country and increases the amount available abroad. This put upward pressure on interest rates in the lending country and downward pressure abroad. Integrated capital markets will then draw credit from the importing countries to the exporting countries to even out the interest rates. The net result is that credit extended abroad to finance foreign buyers is, in a sense, financed by its own credit market.

It is, however, possible for causality to run from the current account to the financial account. Consider the case in which the U.S. suddenly decides to import more. We noted above that this will not lead to a current account deficit because it will be offset by a depreciation of the dollar. Suppose, however, that foreign countries do not want their currencies to appreciate. Their option is to buy the excess dollars in the foreign exchange market. This will be recorded in the financial account as: **foreign official transactions.** Should foreign central banks or treasuries buy U.S. financial assets for whatever reason, the entry would be similarly recorded in the financial account and causality would run from the financial account to the current account.[17]

---

[16] U.S. Trade Deficit Review Commission Final Report, November 14, 2000.
[17] There are a large number of small countries who fix their exchange rate to the U.S. dollar in one way or another. These countries are often in the exchange market to keep their exchange rates fixed. Their purchases and sales of dollars have the same effect on the current account as would occur if the transactor had

Why is the issue of causality important? It is argued that the U.S. trade deficit is of such a magnitude and persistence that it is disruptive to the world economy since it has to be financed by the rest of the world. (Sometimes this argument is levied against China and its large trade surpluses. It was earlier levied against Japan and its trade surpluses.) This objection raises the question of why foreign countries finance the deficit. Why not let the exchange rate depreciate? Most likely, depreciation would be incompatible with the domestic objectives of these countries. They are, after all, sovereign nations with their own economic goals. Economic experts, including Americans, have said that the U.S. current account deficit would go away if the United States would save a larger fraction of its GDP. (The merits of this argument will be discussed in section IV.) This doesn't happen, it is said, because Americans are too addicted to credit and easy living — they don't worry enough about tomorrow and thus save too little.

Alternatively, if causality runs from the financial account to the current account and is driven by the desire of foreign individuals and financial institutions to buy U.S. financial assets, then the case can be made that there is little that can be done about this since the current account deficit is perfectly compatible with equilibrium. The U.S. current account deficit is not disruptive to the world economy and is not being financed by foreigners! Rather, it results from higher yields on U.S. assets or other aspects of the American economy. Americans are not addicted to credit and easy living.

---

been a private entity. There are also countries such as Japan who conduct their monetary policy in the foreign exchange market as perhaps does China. If these countries act to keep their exchange rates constant with the dollar, the data would show that the trade deficit would go hand-in-hand with a largely unchanged dollar exchange rate. This may provide insight into what is causing the trade deficit. If the trade deficit is strongly correlated with real dollar appreciation, causality likely runs from the financial account to the current account. If the trade deficit is weakly correlated with the real exchange rate of the dollar, it is argued, causality likely runs from the current account to the financial account.

C. Does the Current Account Balance Alter the Domestic Money Stock?

Does all this activity in the balance of payments and the foreign exchange market involving billions if not trillions of dollars have any effect on the domestic money supply? Or to put it another way, in the current flexible exchange rate regime used by the United States, do either current account deficits or surpluses have any effect on the outstanding money supply or constrain the ability of the Federal Reserve to conduct monetary policy? The answer is no.[18] To understand why, look at the diagrams above in which only goods and services are bought and sold and the other in which assets are traded. In both, the exchange rate will move to ensure equilibrium meaning that the **supply** of dollars flowing into the foreign exchange market to buy foreign goods, services, and assets is exactly equal to the **demand** for dollars to buy American goods, services, and assets. So the dollars flowing out of the country are equal to the dollars coming in. Moreover, since the Federal Reserve is freed from the requirement to maintain a certain nominal exchange value for the dollar, it can concentrate its attention on achieving its legally mandated goals of full employment and a stable price level.

---

[18] There is one caveat to this conclusion. A large amount of U.S. paper money is foreign-owned. When this amount changes it affects the balance of payments in the very same way as would occur if the currency were part of the interest-bearing government debt.

V. The Model of the Economy

If it is true that the trade deficit is driven by a desire of foreigners to buy American assets because of their higher real yields, one must ask *why* they are higher. And this brings us closer to the ultimate cause of the trade deficit. A compelling reason is that the saving rate of the private and public sectors in the U.S is lower than comparable economies such as Germany, Japan, and China. Thus, to deal with the deficit, if indeed this is desired, fiscal policy should play an important, if not critical role, since government budgets play an important part in the fraction of a country's income that is saved. If the fiscal support is not forthcoming the other measures are a waste of time.[19]

Before conclusions can be reached about sound public policy with regard to the balance of payments, one thing remains to be completed. We must understand how the foreign trade sector integrates into the economy, and for this we will need a model of how the economy works and how its sectors are integrated. Additionally, since international capital flows are sensitive to national interest rates, how the latter are determined is also crucial to an understanding of the balance of payments.

The model developed in this section will be relatively simple. It will consist of three sectors: households plus business or private sector; government or public sector; and foreign trade, or the international sector. We will assume that the economy is at full employment. Why this occurs will be explained (see Appendix E). The three-sector model of the economy will be built one sector at a time in the order laid out above. Once it is completed, public policy options will be presented and worked through. Thus, we begin with a closed economy (one with no international sector and no public sector).

A. Households and Businesses (Private Sector)

A simple economy with only a private sector is shown in Figure 7. For expositional purposes it is divided into households and businesses (these

---

[19] The U.S. experience with fiscal and trade deficits is examined in detail below.

are owned by the households). It depicts the circular flow inherent in all economies, that of income and expenditures. Households supply business with the services of labor and capital. For this they are paid an income (wages and interest) designated as Y. This income is used to meet the current needs and wants of the household sector, some of which are immediate (food, clothing, shelter), others in the future (education of children, retirement, etc.). This use of income is called **consumption** and will be designated as **C** (notice that consumption spending is for non-durable goods and services). The remainder of income not used for Consumption is called **saving** and designated by **Sp** (note *saving* does not refer to saving accounts in banks but is current income not used for consumption). While this saving appears to be done only by households, in fact, some is done by the businesses they own and it is identified separately in the official GDP accounts as **retained earnings** and **depreciation allowances**.

Figure 7
The Circular Flow

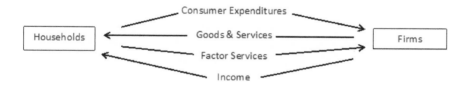

The fraction of income saved by the household (or private) sector need not be a constant. It may be sensitive to the **real rate of interest (r*)** — the evidence for this is scant. The real rate is to be distinguished from the nominal or market rate *i* and is computed as follows. If 100 uniform baskets of goods and services are lent for one year with the promise that the borrower will return 105 uniform baskets one year from now, the real rate will be 5 percent. In general, the real rate can be thought of as the market rate minus the expected rate of inflation (r = i − pe).

Figure 8
Private Sector Saving for a Given Income

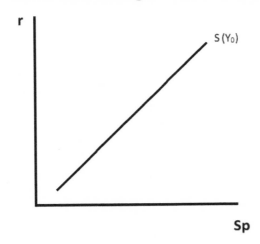

Figure 9
Investment Demand Schedule for Households
(and Businesses)

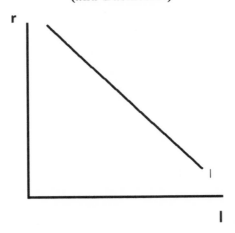

Figure 10
The Determination of the Real Rate of Interest

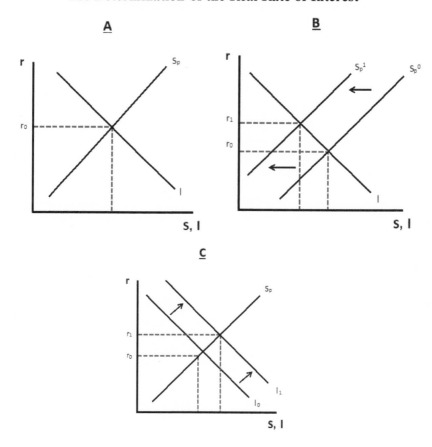

It will be assumed that the fraction of household income saved will be positively related to the real interest rate: the higher the real rate, the larger the quantity of income that is saved. This relationship is shown in Figure 8. How sensitive it is depends on the importance of immediate consumption vs. future consumption. Moreover, as income grows over time, the saving curve will shift to the right.

In addition to using income to gratify immediate needs, households (and businesses) have a need for durable capital goods such as houses, motor vehicles, household durables, plant, equipment, etc. These capital goods will be called investment (I). It will be assumed that for each of

63

these capital goods, households can compute a real rate of return or yield. This computation involves finding the real rate of interest that equates the expected net profit or gain from each capital good with its current price. These can be graphed by their real rate of return from high to low. Such a graph is shown in Figure 9. The I curve is not a constant across time. It can shift right or left depending on expected yields. For example, if households and businesses become more optimistic about the future, the expected profit on capital could improve increasing the expected rate of return. The result would be for the I curve to up or out (generally to the right). Conversely, if pessimism grips them, the expected rate of return is likely to fall, and the curve shifts to the left.

The total expenditures of households or the private sector (E) then consists of C and I. For the circular flow shown in Figure 7 to be in equilibrium, income, or Y must be equal to expenditures, or E. Since Y = C + Sp and E = C + I, Y = E reduces to C + Sp = C + I. Since C occurs on both sides of the equation, it can be cancelled out reducing the equilibrium condition to Sp = I. Thus, the circular flow will continue unchanged so long as the amount households save from income is exactly equal to the desired amount of capital goods households (and businesses) intend to buy. What ensures that this equality will occur? Movements in the real rate of interest. This can be seen when the saving and investment diagrams are combined (Figure 10 A, B, and C). Not only is this the case, but the intersection of the two schedules also determines the equilibrium real interest rate. This same mechanism holds when either or both the S and I schedules change over time.

B. Government (Public Sector)

As shown in Figure 11, governments in most countries do three things that affect the circular flow. They use resources for such things as infrastructure, education, and national security, they transfer income among individuals (think Social Security and Medicare) and they also tax. The entire government budget will enter the circular flow: expenditures for goods and services, transfer payments and taxes. Transfer payments are treated as negative taxes. Adding government also means that household saving and consumption now depend not on income, but on disposable or after tax and transfer income. It will also be sensitive to taxes. It will be assumed that the behavior of the public sector as to expenditures, transfer payments, and taxes is determined by a political process. As a result, Sp can change over time depending on the behavior of political leaders. When this behavior changes, Sp will shift.

Figure 11
Adding the Public Sector to the Circular Flow

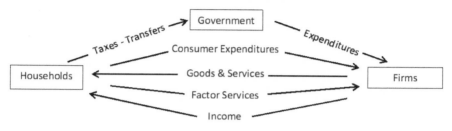

If the government sector runs a budget surplus, it adds to national saving; if it runs a deficit, it reduces national saving. This can be seen from the equation for government saving (budget deficit or surplus): $Sg = (T -$ Government Expenditures), where T = Taxes - Transfers.

An important caveat should be noted. The thrust of fiscal policy is often measured by looking at either the absolute value of the deficit or surplus or the value of each relative to GDP. Reading either as a measure of fiscal thrust can be very misleading. A budget deficit, for example, can occur because tax revenue falls or expenditures and transfers rise. Such changes can occur even if there is no change in tax rates or the formula determining expenditures. External shocks to the economy can reduce income (the tax base) and employment. Such changes to the budget are unlikely to be expansionary. To avoid the inference that they are, economists, in measuring the thrust of fiscal policy, measure the deficit or surplus that would exist if the economy were at full employment [represented as Sg/Yfe]. Changes in this measure of deficit or surplus is the preferred substitute.

The fundamental equation for ensuring that the flows Y and E remain at full employment becomes: $Y = C + Sp + Sg$, $E = C + I$. The two sources of saving can be combined to yield national saving, or $Sn = (Sp + Sg)$. The equilibrium condition for the closed economy then becomes $Sn = I$. As a prelude to looking at the response of an open economy to a shift in fiscal policy, we first look at how it would work itself out in a closed economy

Figure 12
Crowding Out in a Closed Economy

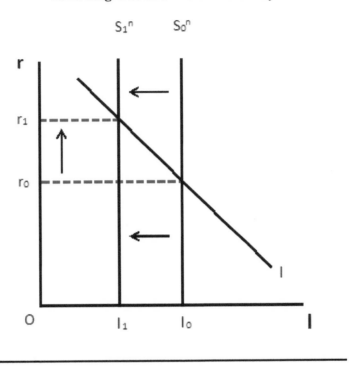

C. From a Closed to an Open Economy (International Sector)

A move from a balanced budget to a budget deficit **[Sn/Yfe]** shown in Figure 12 will, other things equal, shift the Sn curve to the left, raising the real rate of interest and displacing private sector interest sensitive spending. This displacement is known as the **crowding out effect**.[20]

---

[20] How large, depends on whether the changes in the government budget arise from changes in expenditures, transfer payments, or taxes. If taxes, it may affect private sector saving since this depends on after tax income. In addition, changes in taxes can affect the amount of labor and capital supplied to the private sector to produce output. These so-called supply side effects will not be included in the analysis to follow. American experience suggests that they are likely to be small.

Crowding in occurs when the government budget shifts from balance to a surplus. This shifts the Sn curve to the right. How much of each occurs depends on the behavior of the private sector.

Figure 13
The Circular Flow for the Open Economy

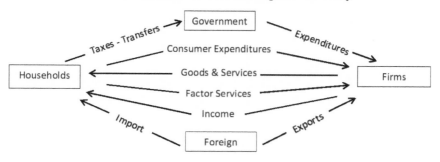

The open economy: The open model, shown in Figure 13, alters the circular flow diagram in two ways: It introduces an additional use of income by adding spending on imports, **M**, and an additional expenditure item, foreign spending on home country output or exports, **X**. These two variables can change over time in response to changes in income, taste and preferences, factor endowments, technologies, and government policies, among others.

The addition of the international sector to the model makes the equilibrium condition a bit more complex. For income and expenditures to remain at full employment we have:

$$C + Sn + M = C + I + X$$

Striking out the C variable on both sides of the equation yields:

$$Sn + M = I + X$$

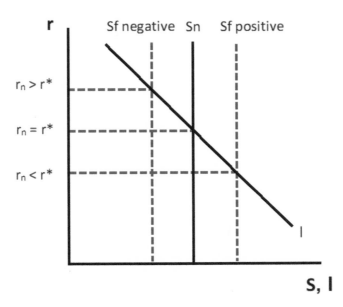

The international portion of this equation [M, X] can be combined in two different ways. First in terms of foreign sector saving or as: $Sf = (M - X)$ and second as net foreign investment or $NFI = (X - M)$.

$$Sn + Sf = Id$$

$Sn = Id - Sf$ and sometimes as: $Sn = Id + NFI$ (or net foreign investment)

When looked at as Sf, it emphasizes that the difference between M and X either adds to or subtracts from the total amount of saving available for investment (Id) in the country. When looked at from the alternative or investment perspective, NFI, it draws attention to the fact the trade balance makes the capital stock of a country larger or smaller than would be the case if the economy were closed. In the following discussion, the emphasis will be on Sf.

Thus, equilibrium reduces to:

$$(1)\ Sn + Sf = Id,\ \text{where}\ Sn = (Sp + Sg)\ \text{or}$$

$$(2)\ Sn = Id + NFI\ [\text{or NX}]$$

My preference is for the first presentation as shown in Figure 14; many textbooks use the second presentation.

This concludes the discussion of the three-sector macro model. It is now time to see how the integrated model responds to fiscal, monetary, and commercial policy changes, some of which are offered to explain Figure 1.

VI. Public Policy Choices

A. Fiscal Policy in the Open Economy

Fiscal policy shifts in a closed economy were analyzed above. In those examples, changing national saving was seen to have an effect on private sector investment. If negative, it was called **crowding out**; if positive, **crowding in**. In the open economy, the nation can, in effect, access foreign saving as can foreign countries access the focus country's saving. Does this render the crowding out or crowding in effect non-operative? Perhaps. It depends critically on how substitutable the financial assets of the focus country are for those in the rest of the world. Several factors suggest why they might be less than perfectly substitutable:

(1) Informational differences. Investors are more likely to understand domestic conditions under which securities are issued and regulated than they are of conditions in other countries. These include simple things like the auditing of financial statements by CPAs or the presentation of government budgets – Greece, for example, was able to conceal its massive fiscal deficits for some years.

(2) Legal restrictions placed on the purchase of foreign securities by U.S. financial institutions. In the U.S., both state and federal laws limit the asset exposure of financial institutions (banks, pension funds, insurance companies) to foreign financial assets.

(3) Exchange rate risk. The investors of any country who buy foreign financial assets denominated in foreign currency expose themselves to a foreign exchange rate risk. What will be the exchange rate when the securities are converted to national currencies?

A.1. Fiscal Expansion and Contraction

As in the closed economy case, fiscal policy changes are measured by changes in the full employment budget deficit or surplus relative to the same measure of GDP. The policy variables: expenditures, transfer payments, and taxes also remain the same. The analysis begins by assuming balanced trade (no net capital transfer or Sf = 0) and balanced budgets across all countries. One new variable is introduced, the world real

70

rate of interest, r^*. This is the real rate determined by a summation of private saving and private investment across all countries. Since the degree of substitutability of financial assets will play a large part in the analysis, three possibilities will be explored:

(a) No substitutability. (the closed economy). The decline in government saving crowds out domestic investment (the case explored above).

(b) Some substitutability. In this case, the domestic real rate has some independence from the world rate. Since it does, fiscal expansion, when it raises the domestic real rate, will draw in some saving or capital from abroad. The local currency will appreciate in the foreign exchange market leading to a trade deficit. The net result will be that crowding out will take the form of a decline in the domestic investment, exports, and import-substitute sectors. All three will experience some loss of output and employment. The sectors that will see increased employment and output depend on what industries benefit from government fiscal action — was it brought about by changes in expenditures, transfer payments, or taxes. Notice also, that in this case the amount of private capital, while subject to some crowding out, will be less than in (a) above. However, the additional capital will be foreign owned and the rewards accruing to this capital will be transferred abroad in the future reducing the income of the host company.

(c) Highly substitutable. In this case, an unchanged world real interest rate, r^*, is imposed on the model. This means that the fiscal action taken by the host country has no effect on the world real rate.[21] As its fiscal shifts put pressure on its domestic interest rate it is swamped by the international movement of saving, both its own and that of foreign countries, which keeps the rate unchanged. In the case of a fiscal deficit, the upward pressure on the domestic interest rate would bring about a net inflow of foreign saving, driving the domestic interest rate back to the world rate. Since the domestic rate will remain unchanged, the net inflow of capital and appreciation of the exchange rate will cause the crowding out to be concentrated exclusively in the international sector of the economy — a fall in exports and contraction in the import competing sector. Notice,

---

[21] There is another possibility and that includes the big country case. In this instance, the financial securities may be perfect substitutes, but the size of the country and its fiscal changes can change the world rate of interest, r^*. To the extent that it can, some of the crowding out or crowding in will be borne by internal investment.

however, that while domestic investment will be unchanged, a portion represented by the trade deficit will be foreign owned, and its factor reward will have to be sent abroad in the future for debt service, reducing the goods and services available to the host economy. In this case, the open economy gives no free lunch from crowding out. While the capital stock will be larger than in the closed economy, the factor income accruing to the domestic owners of capital will be little changed.[22]

Table 7
The Budget Deficit and the Trade Deficit (percent of GDP)

	2008	2009	2010	2011	2012	2013
Budget Deficit	3.6	0.8	0.7	0.6	0.5	0.3
Trade Deficit	5.2	4.1	3.0	3.3	3.3	3.3
	2014	2015	2016	2017	2018	2019
Budget Deficit	0.3	0.2	0.3	0.3	0.4	0.5
Trade Deficit	3.1	3.2	4.0	4.4	4.5	4.0

Sources: Structural budget deficit computed from Congressional Budget Office. Trade deficit and GDP data are from the Department of Commerce.

A.2. The U.S. Experience with Crowding Out

Since the U.S. is a major player in the world economy it is of interest to see the degree to which fiscal expenditures are crowded out by the trade deficit. Much has been made of the twin deficits — the budget and the trade deficits (Figure 1). In Table 7 they are presented for the period years 2009 to 2019, which includes the longest economic expansion in American history. In 4 of the 11 years the two deficits moved in the direction predicted by theory. However, it must be noted that economic theory says this might occur if **"all else is held constant."** Since that is unlikely to be

---

[22] These three cases will also hold to some degree in a less than fully employed economy. Note crowding out will be present whether the economy is fully employed or not. Which sector or sectors will bear the burden of the fall in government saving depends on the substitutability of international financial assets. For a more extensive discussion, see Appendix E.

72

the case, the results in Table 7 should be regarded as suggestive.[23] If we accept what is shown there, a reasonable conclusion would be that a good deal of the budget deficit is offset by the trade deficit and that the U.S. might correspond with case (b) above.

B. Monetary Policy

Thus far, most of the discussion has been carried out with little reference to money and the role the Federal Reserve might play in the balance of payments. Financial assets have been included and how their purchase and sale affects the balance of payments deficits and surpluses analyzed. This discussion has touched on monetary policy. To make this discussion more complete, the role of the Federal Reserve in the balance of payments must be included.

For expositional ease, a flexible exchange rate will be assumed. Later, these issues will be examined in the context of a fixed exchange rate regime for the two regimes impose quite different constraints on the ability of a central bank to manage a nation's money supply.

Monetary policy centers on the actions of the central bank to influence the money and credit conditions in a country. To see how this is done we have to see what determines the money or market rate of interest, i. This, we will see, depends on the demand and supply of money.

A demand for money arises for two reasons: (1) it is a medium of exchange. It is used to make transactions more efficiently than barter; (2) it is also a store of value — that is, it is a highly liquid form in which to hold one's wealth.

Since money is held to make transactions one should expect to see a positive relationship between the volume of expenditures and the amount of money held by the public. Such a relationship is shown in Figure 15.

Since money is also a highly liquid asset, there are a number of reasons why people might want to hold part of their wealth in this form. But holding wealth in the form of money has an opportunity cost: lost income from not holding an interest-earning asset. Thus, the higher the market rate of interest, the less money will be demanded to hold as an asset. This relationship is shown in Figure 16.

---

[23] For the period 1981-2007, see "The Budget Deficit and the Trade Deficit: What is Their Relationship?," Congressional Research Service Report RS21409, August 26, 2008.

In Figure 17, both motives for holding money are combined to form one money demand schedule. The aggregate demand for money shown in Figure 17 is drawn for a given level of expenditures.[24]

In the U.S., the Federal Reserve has the option in conducting monetary policy of using as a target, either the money supply or the market rate of interest. If the target is the former, Figure 18A, the MS curve is vertical (its position on the vertical axis is determined by the amount of money in existence); if the latter, (Figure 18B), it is horizontal at the target interest rate. Our Federal Reserve has chosen as a target a market rate of interest — a very short-term rate known as the Federal Funds Rate — which is the rate that one bank charges another for borrowing bank reserves on an overnight basis.

Figure 15
Transactions Demand for Money

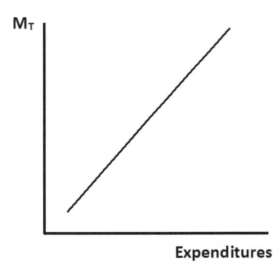

[24] The portion used for transactions is measured on the horizontal axis by the distance from the vertical axis to the point where it parallels the aggregate demand curve.

Figure 16
Money Wealth Holding

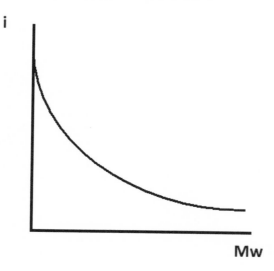

Mw

Figure 17
The Aggregate Demand for Money

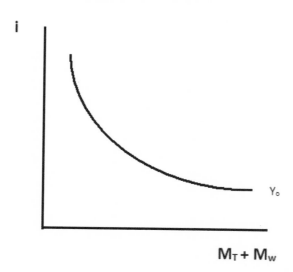

Y_0

$M_T + M_w$

Figure 18
The Demand for and Supply of Money

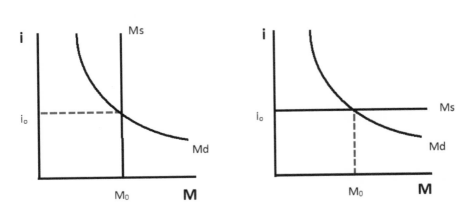

When the central bank wishes to be expansive, it lowers the Federal Funds rate by supplying more reserves to banks on the basis of which they can make more loans thereby easing credit and expanding the supply of money.

B.1. The Monetary Transmission Mechanism

How does changing the market rate of interest and credit conditions change the pace of the economy? Three channels have been identified: (1) interest sensitive domestic spending by households and business; (2) changes in the financial wealth of households which changes their consumption spending;[25] and (3) the international flow of capital, exchange rates, and exports and imports. The importance of the three channels will depend on the substitutability of world financial assets. The greater the substitutability, the greater is the importance of the third channel. To see that this is the case, assume that the central bank brings about an expansion of money and credit by lowering the market interest rate (the Ms schedule shifts out or down in Figure 18). The decrease will

---

[25] Changes in interest rates change the market value of financial assets such as bonds. The reason being is that they change the discounted present value of both the stream of future interest payments from bonds as well as their face value.

stimulate interest-sensitive spending directly and indirectly because the decline will raise the level of financial wealth. This will diminish the desire by households to save and increase consumption spending. It will also decrease the net flow of capital into the focus country (its own citizens will switch from buying domestic financial assets to the now higher yielding foreign assets and foreign citizens will do the same). The reduced inflow (or net outflow) of capital will depreciate the foreign exchange rate, causing exports to rise and imports to fall. The latter will be replaced by an expansion of output from the import substitute industries. The greater the substitutability of financial assets, the more important channel 3 is in transmitting monetary policy changes to changes in aggregate spending. This occurs because small changes in the domestic interest rate will bring about large and immediate changes in the net flow of international capital and, because they are small, will have a limited effect on increased spending from channels 1 and 2.

B.2. Does Monetary Policy Involve Exporting Unemployment?

What will be evident from monetary policy shifts will be an immediate and visible effect on the exchange rate. The focus country will see its exchange rate depreciate while recipient countries will see their exchange rates appreciate. It won't take the recipients long to realize what this means for the export and import competing sectors of their economies. The cry will go up that they are the victims of **currency manipulation,** the purpose of which is to export the initiating country's unemployment to them. Such a policy, they are also likely to add, is directed at destroying vital sectors of their economy — usually manufacturing, with its high-paying jobs. What will pass without comment is that the monetary policy change set in motion the export of capital or the saving of the focus country and that the inflow of that saving to them made possible a larger capital stock than would otherwise have taken place.

Whether net unemployment will be exported is uncertain. Clearly the nature of employment is likely to change. Both labor and capital will be re-orientated. The United States frequently makes this charge against China, among other countries. The U.S. Treasury is required twice a year to evaluate the behavior of exchange rates of a number of countries and come to a conclusion about whether they offer evidence sufficient to brand a country as a manipulator. Thus far, China has not been so branded. Nevertheless, both Democrats and Republicans pressure the Treasury to change its mind since, according to them, China is responsible for the decline of the U.S manufacturing sector. (See below for a more extended discussion of this topic.)

Prior to China, the ire of American politicians was directed against the economic policies of Japan. Japan ran a very large bilateral trade surplus with the United States for many years. At the same time, Japanese motor vehicles were a large and growing part of the trade with the United States. The volume of complaints against Japanese economic policy seemed highly correlated with increases in its share of the U.S. auto market. The question arose in U.S. policy circles as to whether Japan was actively involved in manipulating the dollar-yen exchange rate. These exchange rate changes might have been due largely to the fact that Japan could not conduct monetary policy in the traditional way. In the case of the U.S. the exchange rate is a residual that results from the Federal Reserve conducting monetary policy by fixing domestic interest rates. The interest rate is the target and the exchange rate the residual. In the case of Japan, the interest rate cannot be the target as for many years the short-term rate and even the long-term rate have been too low to be used as an effective target, especially if the central bank wanted to ease monetary conditions. Since capital mobility is high in the case of Japan, if the interest rate were the target, the principal channel of monetary policy would be the exchange rate. So why not target the exchange rate directly? In this case, the exchange rate becomes a non-residual, but only in the special case where the market interest rates are too low to effectuate monetary policy. Thus, in Japan, the foreign exchange market becomes the market in which monetary policy is carried out.

There are a large number of relatively small countries that fix their exchange rate to the U.S. dollar or to a market basket of goods in which the dollar has a large weight. Some do this to achieve a low inflation rate, while in others it is a part of a more comprehensive economic plan to achieve a range of goals related to employment, GDP growth, and inflation. From time to time it may be necessary to change the exchange rate target. They are, after all, sovereign states whose policies are designed for the betterment of their own citizens. One should be reluctant to brand them as currency manipulators. Their central banks are no different from the Federal Reserve, whose monetary conduct is to achieve the goals of full employment and low inflation imposed on it by the U.S. Congress. Indeed, on this basis, it could be claimed that the Federal Reserve is an interest rate manipulator.

VII. Other Alleged Causes of the Trade Deficit

In this section, alternative explanations for the trade deficit are considered in terms of the full model of the economy to highlight the need for a disparity between domestic saving and investment to enable a sustained trade deficit to exist. Without this disparity, these allegations are without merit.

A. The Imposition of Trade Barriers

In an example above, the imposition of a trade impediment such as a tariff or quota was done in the expectation that it might increase employment. The example assumed balanced trade and concluded that the impediment would not lead to a trade surplus but balanced trade at a lower level of trade. Those who thought otherwise did so because they neglected the exchange rate change. Does the conclusion change when considered in the context of the open economy model? The answer is no. A trade surplus (or deficit) can only exist if offset by a net movement of capital. Without this, trade must be balanced. All the impediment does is to reduce the volume of trade. And as before, a tax on imports is also an equivalent tax on exports. This conclusion bears on a central goal of Mercantilism: a country should conduct trade so as to annually sell to foreigners more than it buys from them. The wisdom of Thomas Mun is no wisdom at all. Thus, changes in commercial policy are not the road to increased employment.[26]

B. Developing and/or Expanding New Markets Abroad

A frequent political theme in the U.S. (and an early *raison d'être* for the Department of Commerce) is to create new or expand existing foreign markets as a means of job creation. Often the political eye is cast longingly

---

[26] In 1931, as the U.S. economy was collapsing, Congress enacted the Smoot-Hawley Tariff Act, which increased tariffs on more than half of U.S. imports. President Hoover signed the tariff bill on the basis that American labor faced unfair competition from cheap labor abroad. The act did little if anything to stabilize or reverse the rise in unemployment. Historians have attached the word *infamy* to this tariff.

at South America. While expanding trade has many virtues, using it as a means for increasing employment is unlikely to be one of them. The adage, goods and services pay for goods and services applies here. If through trade promotion, the U.S. sells more abroad, the induced change in the exchange rate neglected by these proponents will ensure that additional imports will be forthcoming from these countries unless the increased exports are accompanied by an increase in the net export of capital and this is possible only if national saving exceeds domestic investment. A variation on this theme is to get countries with whom the U.S. has a bilateral trade deficit to buy more America goods. For reasons explained above this in and of itself won't do the job.

C. Bad Trade Deals

A constant refrain from the Trump administration is that the U.S. trade deficit shown in Figure 1 results from bad trade deals. Either the U.S. is taken advantage of or nefarious foreigners sell us things based on technology stolen from us or use it to undermine our markets abroad. Such a conclusion is wrong on two counts. First, since 1970 the U.S. has had only three years in which the trade balance has been positive. (Much of this period was long before NAFTA, claimed by President Trump to be the worst trade deal in American history — fewer than 500,000 displaced workers have filed for job retraining.) It is unlikely that any country would have been so incompetent for so long. Second, a trade deficit can only exist if the U.S. has been a net importer of capital. That is, it has been a net recipient of foreign capital. Its domestic saving, Sn, has been less than the sum of Sn + Sf. Without this, the trade deficit could not exist regardless of how incompetent its trade negotiators.

D. Has the Trade Deficit Cost the U.S. Jobs?

This claim is related to C above. Again, the answer is two-fold. If it has cost the U.S jobs, it must have been in the millions since our trade accounts have only been in surplus for three years since 1970. From the analysis above, the job loss, if any, is uncertain. The macro model tells us that the net inflow of saving from abroad, which makes the trade deficit possible, adds to the capital stock of the country, thereby creating jobs in the capital goods industries while it bears negatively on the export and import-competing sectors of the economy, causing job losses there. The net employment results are uncertain.

E. Changes in the World Real Rate of Interest, r^*

The rate at which various countries save or invest is likely to change across time. Moreover, a growing number of countries enter (and some leave) the world financial community. All this implies that the world rate of saving and investment is unlikely to remain fixed. As they change, so does the world real interest rate r^*. How do these changes affect a country's balance of payments? To answer this question, assume a high degree of financial integration and that r^* falls as the world saves a larger portion of its income (either or both private and public sector saves more), and countries whose rate is now above the new r^* will find themselves selling their now higher-yielding securities to those countries whose yield is lower. The net inflow of capital (saving) will cause the exchange rate to appreciate, leading to a fall in exports and a shift to imports from domestically produced substitutes. Beginning from balanced trade, the country will have a trade deficit. The increased employment in the capital good sector will be countered by the loss of employment in the foreign trade sector. China has an unusually high rate of national saving. As it began to open its economy to the world, one might have predicted that some portion of these saving would find their way into the world economy, altering the saving-investment balance of other nations. This alteration would then affect the real exchange rate and the structure of employment in these countries as explained above. The United States has been one of the countries that has received a large inflow of saving from China and has caused a large amount of discord between the two nations.

F. Changes in Tastes and Preferences

Suppose the consumers in a country change from preferring imported goods to substitutes produced at home. What will be the effects on the home economy? The change will reduce the amount of money supplied to the foreign exchange market appreciating the home country currency (the S curve in Figure 2 will shift to the left). The appreciation will reduce the quantity of exports so that trade is once again balanced. This must happen, since the change in tastes had no effect on aggregate consumption or saving in the private sector. Notice, however, that it will change the nature

81

of employment, requiring a transition of labor and capital from the export sector to the import-competing sector. (Studies exist that suggest that the adjustment of labor is more complex in the sense that labor displaced by trade changes seldom moves from the export to import-competing sectors and vice versa.)

A change in preferences may also apply to financial assets. Newly emerging markets in foreign countries, discoveries of new natural resources or methods of extraction, declines in risks, etc., may attract the interests of the capitalist. If they affect the net international flow of capital, they will affect the trade balance leading either to a net outflow or inflow.

G. Different National Growth Rates

The amount of foreign trade depends not only on the prices of imports and export but on how fast nations grow. If two nations spend the same proportion of their income on imports, then differential growth rates will, other things held constant, lead to continuous pressure for unbalanced trade. It will also mean a continuous net inflow of money from the faster growing country into the foreign exchange market leading to a depreciation of its currency in order to restore equilibrium. It will not lead to unbalanced trade. There may, however, be an exception. If the differential growth rates reflect such things as technology differences that may change the relative rates of yield on capital, it may alter the net international flow of capital, which can cause a trade surplus or deficit.

H. New Nations Join the World Trading Community

Two memorable events toward the end of the twentieth century that have had a profound effect on the world economy were the collapse of the Soviet Union and the decision by China to become a major player in the world economy. These changes produced both opportunities and problems for the affected countries. One major consequence was a dramatic change in the factor proportions of the trading world and the comparative advantage of many countries. Some of these involving shifts in comparative advantage should be sorted out by appropriate changes in the structure of the real exchange rates of the various countries without causing trade imbalances. However, some, such as analyzed in E. above can lead to an imbalance in trade.

There have been several other shifts in the world that merit discussion and these involve the discovery of new resources. In 1959, a very large deposit of natural gas was discovered in the Netherlands (the Groningen field) sufficient to make that country energy independent and, as a consequence, reducing its imports significantly. The result was a substantial appreciation of the Dutch guilder that worked a great hardship on the export sector of the country. The *Economist* magazine introduced the term "Dutch Disease" to describe this mixed blessing and so it is used to this day. There were more such discoveries: oil in Siberia that turned the Soviet Union into an oil exporter and, according to historians, prolonged the life of that regime; the discovery of oil in the North Sea in the 1980s adjacent to the United Kingdom and Norway, making each energy independent, and the technologies making fracking possible, which shifted the United States from an oil importing to an oil exporting country. All the discoveries caused exchange appreciations not quite of the magnitude of the Dutch guilder. These did not lead to trade surpluses for the relevant countries.

I. Firms Move Production to Other Countries

Many firms that engage in international commerce have an evolutionary cycle. They often begin with exporting from their country of domicile through sales offices located in the countries where they sell their goods and services. As these markets expand, it often becomes more efficient to set up limited production subsidiaries (GM Buick in China) to service these markets. Additional growth often merits still more off-shore production, and the subsidiaries become fully vertically integrated firms. At each stage of this evolution, exports from the focus country tend to be replaced by production abroad. Sometimes, costs of labor are cheaper than at home. The displaced factors will appeal to their governments to do something about it. To support their case for intervention, the displaced factors will argue that this practice contributes to the trade deficit. Their argument is incorrect. Since goods pay for goods, the replacement of exports by production abroad will cause the exchange rate to appreciate, reducing imports from the country benefiting from the offshoring.[27]

---

[27] For an early attempt to measure the effect of U.S. direct investment abroad on the U.S. balance of payments, see Gail Makinen. "The Pay-Off Period of Direct

J. The Absence of a Level Playing Field

It is often asserted that America's trade difficulties come from the fact that American exporters face higher tariffs and other trade restrictions than foreigners face when they sell in the U.S. As an example, U.S. tariffs on automobiles are about 2.5 percent whereas foreign tariffs on U.S. automobiles run about 10 percent. Is it any wonder then that America has a trade deficit when American sellers are placed at such a competitive disadvantage? All we ask, the American competitor says, is a level playing field where all countries impose the same rate of taxes and the same trade restrictions. As intuitive as this argument sounds, an un-level playing field will not produce a trade deficit. It will affect the composition and the level of trade. Why is this so? It arises from the simple proposition that in the absence of a net exchange of financial assets, trade in goods and services must be equal. The imposition or reduction of trade barriers will alter the amount and the composition of what is traded, but the exchange rate will adjust to maintain balance between exports and imports. So, while specific American businesses may be injured by the disparity in import taxes, other American firms benefit from the exchange rate change it brings about. And, of course, the foreigners who must pay a higher tariff are injured, especially their export industries.

K. Repatriation of Earnings and Domestic Employment

Related to J. above is the argument for lowering U.S. taxes on repatriated retained earnings that American foreign subsidiaries currently hold abroad. This amount has been calculated to be in the hundreds of billions of dollars, and great promise was held out that it would be used by their domestic parents on new investment in the U.S. that would lead to the creation of thousands of new jobs. Unfortunately, this is unlikely to happen. While it is undoubtedly true that large amounts are held abroad by American subsidiaries, they are not held in the form of assets denominated in term of dollars. They are held as euros, pounds, yen, etc. To realize these assets in terms of dollars, they must first go through the foreign exchange market. This will increase the demand for dollars and

---

Foreign Investment of the United States Automotive Industry," *Journal of Business*, October 1970.

cause the dollar to appreciate in terms of foreign currencies, making foreign goods cheaper in the U.S. and raise the price of American goods abroad. The net result is a trade deficit. This exercise is exactly the same as the one above in which foreigners decide to invest in the United States. To do so, they must first acquire dollars.

L. The Effects of Trade on the U.S. Manufacturing Sector

Perhaps the most vocal argument for trade barriers is that foreign trade has wiped out the manufacturing sector of the U.S. economy with a massive loss of good paying jobs and is causing much distress to families and communities where these jobs were once plentiful. To evaluate this argument, the data on which it is based must be examined. The first prerequisite is to define what subsectors are included in Manufacturing. They are shown in Table 8.

Second, the value of this output must be determined. Three methods exist to estimate the gross output of the United States. The first and most common is Gross Domestic Product. GDP measures the end uses made of national output: consumption, investment, government, and exports. Since a purely domestic measure is desired, imports are subtracted. The second method is to add up the amount paid to each factor of production (rent, wages, salaries, profits, and interest) to produce the nation's output. A third, but seldom used measure, is to look at the amount of output or value added by the various sectors of the economy, one of which is manufacturing.

Those who argue that the U.S. is being deindustrialized for some reason want to use the nominal value of the output of the manufacturing sector relative to the nominal value of GDP. The result, shown in Figure 19, produces the striking conclusion that the U.S. is, indeed, being deindustrialized and, not surprisingly, being matched by a precipitous decline in employment in that sector also shown on the same figure. The villain in the piece supposedly is international trade or globalization.

Why one would want to use the nominal measure of output is curious. No serious economist would measure the growth rate of any country using nominal GDP. Rather, the real or deflated value of GDP would be used. And, indeed, when the real measure of output by the manufacturing sector relative to real GDP is used, it shows, in the same figure, little or no trend in the relative size of the manufacturing sector since the end of World War II. That size, however, displays a cyclical pattern, as one might expect since the output of durable goods (think motor vehicles) is more likely to decline in recessions than nondurables (think food).

Table 8
The Composition of Manufacturing by Subsector

1. Food Manufacturing
2. Beverage and Tobacco Product Manufacturing
3. Textile mills
4. Textile Product Mills
5. Apparel Manufacturing
6. Leather and Allied Product Manufacturing
7. Wood Product Manufacturing
8. Paper Manufacturing
9. Printing and Related support Activities
10. Petroleum and Coal Products Manufacturing
11. Chemical Manufacturing
12. Plastics and Rubber Products Manufacturing
13. Nonmetallic Mineral Products Manufacturing
14. Fabricated Metal Product Manufacturing
15. Machinery Manufacturing
16. Computer and Electronic Product Manufacturing
17. Electronic Equipment, Appliances, and Component Manufacturing
18. Transportation Equipment Manufacturing
19. Furniture and Related Product Manufacturing
20. Miscellaneous Manufacturing

Thus, the argument that the U.S. has become deindustrialized is simply not true. Employment in the manufacturing sector has declined both absolutely and relative to the labor force, but this is primarily due to the substitution of capital and technology for labor. What the data tell us is a story about a very large rise in labor productivity in manufacturing, not the ill effects of globalization.[28]

---

[28] For an excellent discussion of the U.S. manufacturing sector, see Martin Neil Baily and Barry P. Bosworth, "U.S. Manufacturing: Understanding Its Past and Its Potential Future," *Journal of Economic Perspectives,* Winter 2014: 3-26.

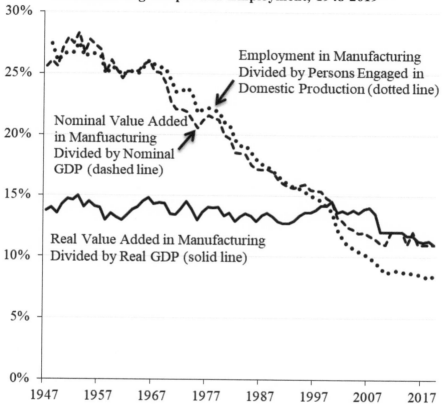

Figure 19
Manufacturing Output and Employment, 1948-2019[29]

Source: U.S. Department of Commerce, Bureau of Economic Analysis, and U.S Department of Labor

---

[29] The data used in this figure are not consistent across time. The definition of both real manufacturing output and employment in manufacturing changed. The new data for the former began in 2009, but it was extended back to 1987. Thus, the period 1987-2009 can be compared using both definitions. They show that the definitional changed reduced the size of the manufacturing sector, but not the pattern of its change over time. It continues to have a strong relationship with real GDP. Similarly, the number of individuals employed in the manufacturing sector also declined, but not by much. In this instance, we have three years of data measuring employment using both definitions.

M. The Mercantilistic Policies of China

The spectacular economic transformation of China since the early 1980s and its decision to open itself to trade with the rest of the world was bound to be upsetting to the economies of many countries including the United States as it must have altered the comparative-advantage least-comparative disadvantage basis for their trade. Moreover, the high saving rate of China meant that it could be a source of world capital should it choose to be so. If it did, it meant that China would run a trade surplus with a number of countries, including the United States. When this came to pass, China's economic policies were tainted with the word "Mercantilistic" just as those of Japan were before China took center stage. What exactly were the sins of China? It built excess steel capacity to drive American steel companies out of business. It built its industries by stealing U.S. trade secrets. It forced U.S. companies who wanted to set up operations in China to partner with a Chinese company. The Chinese company would then plunder the technology from its American partner and, once achieved, break the partnership. China bought into U.S. companies to steal their technology. International companies dependent on Chinese trade were under pressure from the Communist party to abandon their liberal values, forgo criticism, and provided at least tacit support for the repression of the Chinese people. And the list goes one.

Whether these assertions are valid or not, the important issue is how to deal with them. If these practices violate U.S. patents or copyrights, a legal remedy is available. That route does not seem to have been taken. Rather, the one taken by the U.S. government has involved withdrawing from multinational trade pacts to which China is a member; imposing sanctions on Chinese companies which limit the business they can do in the U.S. and tariffs on import competing Chinese products, including steel and various durable goods used by American households; and accusing the Chinese government of currency manipulation to undervalue the yuan to make Chinese goods cheap in the U.S., thereby creating the bilateral trade deficit.

Recall from the discussion above, trade barriers that reduce U.S. imports will have a negative effect on U.S exports.[30] This is clearly evident

---

[30] The reduction in exports is due primarily to a change in the real exchange rate, but there is also a second effect. Since a good deal of American imports are not

in the distress experienced by U.S. farmers following the 2020 U.S. tariffs on Chinese goods. The U.S. government's response was a huge income transfer from American taxpayers to American farmers. Thus, Americans paid twice for this policy — they pay a higher price for what they consume and they pay higher taxes to compensate American farmers for the injury done to them by the government's policy choice.

Absent from much of public discussion is the fact that U.S. interest rates have been at historic lows even during the run up to the longest economic expansion in U.S. history. Could this be due to the large inflow of Chinese capital into the U.S.? China is a large holder of U.S. government interest-bearing debt. Observers looking at this buildup are likely to claim that it is evidence for currency manipulation. But it cannot be denied that Chinese saving are being transferred to the U.S. by this purchase of interest-bearing debt. China's relations with the U.S. are complex, but good economic policies should not be cast aside without serious thought.

N. Loss of International Competitiveness

The size and continued persistence of the U.S. trade deficit has given rise to a recurring theme: The U.S. is no longer competitive internationally. The vague nature and opaqueness of the term makes for a difficult definition. It has no meaning in terms of the theory of comparative advantage unless it is taken to mean that the U.S has continued to lose comparative advantage in the goods and services it produces and increasingly depends for trade on the things in which it has a least comparative disadvantage. There is no doubt that the composition of U.S. trade has changed over time. But this does not mean that such changes alter the gains from trade or bring in their wake a trade deficit. The latter still depends on the net saving position of a nation.

O. The Balance of Payments Deficit and the Exchange Rate Regime

Earlier it was noted that the beginning of the long history of balance of payments deficits coincided with the U.S. change from a fixed to a

---

finished goods, but components and parts, it increases production costs in the U.S. of products that use these imports which can have additional trade implications.

flexible exchange regime. Is this merely a coincidence, or do we see a cause and effect relationship? A number of economists and financial commentators see the latter, but fall short explaining why this relationship should exist. Most of the reasons given, covered above, will not cause balance of payments deficits. The difficulty of linking the changes is that in an important sense the exchange rate change was forced. The post-World War II global monetary standard was a dollar standard. Countries fixed their exchange rates to the dollar and the dollar was fixed to gold at $35 per troy ounce. The U.S. promised gold redemption to official dollar holders. The decades after the war were ones of "dollar shortage." European countries could not get enough dollars to rebuild their destroyed economies. That being the case, the accumulation of dollar reserves abroad did not constrain U.S. policy. As Europe recovered and dollar holdings by foreign central banks continued to rise, dollar shortage gave wave to dollar glut and the U.S. was faced with the prospect that its gold holdings were insufficient to honor large-scale demands by foreign central banks for conversion. When this began to happen in the early 1970s, the U.S. had little choice but to devalue the dollar. When the run on U.S. gold reserves continued, the U.S. refused to redeem the holdings of central banks and the dollar was allowed to float.

Given this history, it becomes difficult to recast, what might have happened had the dollar standard continued. Worries about dollar conversion by foreign central banks might have constrained U.S. foreign policy (a major reason for the avalanche of dollars sent abroad) and domestic policy. But it is doubtful that the old dollar standard could have continued for more three-quarters of a century after the end of World War II Thus, it is hard to make a convincing case that the regime change had anything to do with the continuous balance of payments deficit.

VIII. Summary and Conclusions

Public policy decisions with regard to the balance of payments should be based on a model consistent with the efficient use of resources and the maximization of consumer choices. This is more likely to be the case with an industrial policy in which free trade plays a major role rather than one in which winners and losers are selected and the resultant resource allocation is determined primarily by a process that reflects the wishes or desires of politicians, elected or otherwise.

However decisions are made, they must contend with several simple notions that have profound implications for policy choices. Two are particularly important. First, in the absence of the net international movement of financial assets, the goods and services sold abroad by a nation must be equal to the goods and services that it buys from abroad. Second, when a net movement of financial assets occurs, the country that is the net buyer of those assets must have an excess of national saving over domestic investment. Sadly, the incorporation of these notions into public policy discussions is largely absent. Equally sad, is the absence of any acknowledgement that policy decisions affect the exchange rate. It is as though all these decisions have, are, and will take place in an area that uses the same money. International borders seem to be nonexistent. The result of a neglect of these three notions is that public policy decisions made to accomplish a given end adversely affect other sectors of the economy, don't accomplish their intended goals, and do great harm to the well-functioning and political harmony of the world economy.

The notable American economist Paul Samuelson famously observed that every economy has to solve three basic questions: what to produce, how to produce it, and to whom shall the output be distributed. The international exchange of goods and services and the movement of the factors of production across national boundaries may add a fourth fundamental question: Where are the goods and services produced?

There have been two quite different approaches to the "where" question. For many years, government played an active role in answering it. This period was labelled Mercantilism, and it reached its apogee in 19th century Britain. The answer to this question was governed by a simple goal for a state: produce and conduct trade so as to achieve as large and positive a balance of payments surplus as possible. As a counterpart, trade deficits were frowned upon and something to be avoided as dangerous. These notions set the parameters for public policy related to international trade for many nations. An alternative arose to challenge Mercantilism. It consisted of an explanation for why this goal was both unachievable for individual nations and for all of them simultaneously. By explaining why trade takes place and the benefits from it for all participant nations, it suggested a menu of policies that would enhance the well-being of all nations. Unfortunately, Mercantilism never died. Remnants still exist. In the United States, its adherents now use the term "reshoring" and march under the banner: "Buy American, hire American, and make it in the USA." The fact that such a policy will injure many other Americans seems of little concern. Sound public policy should not be based on doing harm to others.

Appendices

A. Assumptions of the Smith-Ricardo and Heckscher-Ohlin Models

The two basic models that make the case for free trade, Smith-Ricardo and H-O, do so based on a variety of assumptions. Smith-Ricardo assume the goods and services produced by the two countries are identical, there is only one factor of production (labor), and it is qualitatively the same across all countries, perfectly mobile internally and perfectly immobile externally. It is indifferent as to which sector it works in and, as a result, the real wage is the same in both sectors.

Both Smith and Ricardo adhere to the labor theory of value prevalent at that time, which held that the exchange value of a good or service is determined by the amount of labor needed to produce it, e.g., eight hours. Both recognized that capital goods existed, but capital intensive or indirect methods of production have no advantage over direct methods. Therefore, capital used in production merely transferred to the good or service the amount of labor it took to produce the capital. Thus, if it took 100 hours of labor to build the capital and the capital goods depreciated to zero after 10 units of goods or services were produced, each unit would then contain 10 units of labor in exchange for other goods and services. This meant that the price of the good was supply determined — in economic terms, the marginal cost to produce each product was constant and, hence, the supply curve of output was horizontal. There were no scale economies, and technology considerations were assumed not to exist. While tastes and preferences, the determinants of demand, could be different, they played no role in pre-trade price determination. The only role they (or demand) played was to determine the level of output of the two goods.

However, after trade opened, tastes and preferences played the major role in determining the after-trade exchange rate of the two goods. Before trade (and after), both countries were at full employment, although after trade the type of employment would change as each country would specialize in the good or service in which it had a comparative advantage or least comparative disadvantage. This meant that they assumed perfect mobility of labor internally and complete immobility between countries. The market structure was that of perfect competition (each firm produced to the point at which price = marginal cost).

The H-O model is different from Smith-Ricardo in the assumption of multi-factors of production, a contemporary theory of price determination in which both supply (cost of production) and demand (utility) determine pre-trade prices (hence, scale economies are important and produce upward sloping supply curves). However, in order to conclude that relative factor endowments determine trade, they must assume that tastes and preference are identical across countries and this will yield similar demand curves for both goods and services in the two countries.

B. How to Read the Financial Section of Newspapers

The financial sections of newspapers are a rich source of information about the economy, its history, and forecasts for the future. Many of these articles are written by journalists who do not have a professional background as economists. If they (and a large number of other professional people) were asked the simple question: "What would you expect to happen to the quantity of coffee consumed if you saw the price of coffee rise?" Expectation is that the vast majority would answer in one word: decline. And they might be correct. However, they could be wrong. In making their forecast, they are implicating assuming that there is a net decrease in the supply of coffee — or in other words, the supply curve is shifting backward. They could be wrong. If the demand curve for coffee shifted outward it would produce a rising price of coffee and a rising consumption of coffee. Only by looking at the consumption of coffee over time, can see what answer is correct.

Similarly, the financial press is replete with articles with such headlines as "Watch Out for a Bigger Trade Gap" (displaying two graphs; one a rising real value of the dollar and the other a trade gap that is growing). The thrust of the article is that the rising real value of the dollar will cause a further increase in the trade gap. This may not be the case. To come a conclusion about trade gap, you must first understand why dollar is appreciating.

Economists distinguish between variables that are **exogenous** and **endogenous**. The former are given *to* the system while the latter are determined *by* the system. In the coffee example above, the price of coffee is an endogenous variable and is determined by both the supply and demand for coffee, and both must be considered before a conclusion can be drawn. To take the price of coffee as predetermined (exogenous or given to the system) and then conclude what happens when the price rises can lead to mistakes. Read the newspaper carefully!

C. Supply and Demand in the Foreign Exchange Market

The demand and supply schedules introduced in Figure 2 have the shape usually presented in text books. In the foreign exchange market, this need not be the case. For this to be so, the elasticity of demand for the goods and services of HOME and FOREIGN must not be too inelastic or unresponsive to changes in the price of what they import. In the text it was stated that as the exchange rate appreciates, for examples, HOME, will spend more on what it imports whilst FOREIGN will spend less. For this to be true, the quantity demanded must increase (decrease) by more than the fall (rise) in price. To see why, consider the extreme case where the elasticity of demand in HOME for the goods of FOREIGN is zero – that is, the demand curve is a straight vertical line for these products. Exchange rate appreciation or depreciation will not alter the quantity demanded. Under these circumstances, the amount of its' money HOME will supply to the foreign exchange market will fall as its' currency appreciates. As a result, the supply of foreign exchange will slope downward and to the right — both supply and demand will slope the same way. Will they cross to determine an equilibrium price? This possibility has intrigued economists and two of them, Alfred Marshall and Abba Lerner, specified the conditions under which this will occur.[31] Thus, the conclusion emerges that the elasticity of the demand and supply curves in the foreign exchange market depend on the elasticity of demand in both HOME and FOREIGN for the goods and services they import and this will be heavily influenced by the availability of substitutes.

D. An Evaluation of Flexible and Fixed Exchange Regimes

Adjustments to economic shocks: As noted above, the crucial exchange rate for responding to economic shocks is the real rate and the two regimes accomplish this in quite different ways. In the case of a nominally fixed rate, the price levels in the countries must change. What happens if they do not adjust rapidly, as is likely to be the case, as most

---

[31] Marshall worked on a solution to this problem in the 19th century and years later Lerner refined his work.

prices (including wages) are not determined in auction markets. That is, the majority of them will be sticky, as they are often determined by contract or the menu cost associated with changing them. Thus, in the case of a country with a trade deficit, its income will have to decline to restore balance to the trade account. The country with a trade surplus will get a net boost to demand. If this threatens inflation, its central bank and/or treasury have the means to thwart this development. But clearly the pressure will be on the country with the trade deficit to restore balance. And this brings us to the (perverse) behavior expected of central bankers in this system. The central bankers in the trade-deficit country are expected to allow the income of the country to fall to restore balance, something that will likely be resisted by the political leadership of the country. The central bankers in the country with a surplus are expected to allow prices to rise, something its political leadership is likely to resist. If either the fall in income or the rise in prices is expected to be large, pressure will build among politicians to change the exchange rate either through devaluation or revaluation to restore equilibrium.

Policy goals: It is common practice for countries to set goals for their economic policies. In a flexible exchange-rate regime, both monetary and fiscal policy can be used to achieve price level stability and high employment. In a fixed regime this is not the case. The central bank can have but one goal: keep the nominal exchange rate unchanged to gold, silver, the U.S. dollar, etc. This goal can also constrain fiscal policy in that it must be consistent with the exchange rate goal. Thus, one can argue that in the flexible exchange-rate regime internal stability is purchased with the possibility of external instability, while in the fixed regime internal stability is sacrificed for external stability.

The system anchor: A variation on the goal independence theme, is one made in terms of a system anchor. The fixed regime is anchored to gold, dollars, etc. which constrains both monetary and fiscal policies which, it is argued, is conductive to economic growth. While flexible regimes have no such anchor, they are, in fact, anchored by the goals set by the government. In the U.S., the law mandates a stable price level and high employment. The history of these two regimes does not provide a clear picture as to which is better in terms of producing stable prices and high employment. One can pick and choose the time period. One fact does stand out: fixed exchange-rate regimes do not guarantee a fixed nominal rate over time. They are replete with official changes, both devaluations and appreciations. During the 20th century, the U.S. devalued the dollar twice (1934 and 1973). The fact that a majority of international trade and finance is carried out by countries that adhere to the flexible rate regimes speaks to their popularity.

The cost to run these systems: Fixed exchange rate regimes can be expensive to run. They require reserve holdings. Government taxes are used to acquire the reserve asset. Flexible regimes do not require assets holdings since market adjustments ensure exchange equilibrium. Some countries do, however, hold reserves to smooth fluctuations.

Exchange rate risks that inhibit trade: A great deal of international trade is not done on a cash and carry basis. Rather, contracts are used. If only the currencies of the parties to a contract are used, one party will not know with certainty what must be paid. Some of this uncertainty can be reduced if not eliminate by using the forward exchange market. But the additional risk is thought to inhibit the growth of trade. Given the robust growth of international trade and commerce in the post-World War II era, the effect of this risk appears to be minimal.

Growth of anchor unpredictable: For a fixed exchange rate to function well, the growth of the anchor (gold, dollars, etc.) should expand as the demand for reserves expands. If it does not, the world economy will experience either an inflationary or deflationary bias. There is no certainty that this will occur.

Speculation: One problem that history reveals with fixed regimes is that they are subject to speculation whenever there is doubt that the exchange rate peg cannot be maintained. A major bout occurred in the late 1990s, when a number of Asian countries that had pegged their exchange rate to the dollar were put under pressure to appreciate their currencies as the dollar rose in real terms against the major currencies. This would have required them to bring about a fall in their price levels. Speculators guessed correctly that this would not happen and that they would devalue — they were mostly right.

E. The Assumption of Full Employment

One of the important policy shifts discussed in the text involved fiscal policy. In the discussion about how these shifts affected the economy, full employment was assumed. Our interests centered on the "crowding out" effect. In the closed economy, changes in fiscal policy were seen to cause offsetting changes in private investment. Fiscal expansion, measured by changes in the full employment measure of the budget, leads to an equal decline in private investment, whereas fiscal contraction leads to an offsetting rise in private investment. In the open economy case, the offset could also occur in the foreign trade sector with fiscal expansion leading to a trade deficit and contraction a trade surplus. The degree to which the fiscal shifts were concentrated in the foreign trade sector depended on the degree to which international capital markets were integrated — the more substitutable the financial assets of one nation were for the others, the greater was crowding out concentrated in the foreign trade sector. The reason for assuming full employment is to get the direction and maximum offsetting effect from the fiscal shift. However, fiscal shifts are seldom undertaken in conditions of full employment. The stabilization role performed by fiscal shifts is to return an economy to a full employment growth path. In the process, they affect income and interest rates which affects private investment and the foreign trade sector. And these income changes can mute the magnitude of the crowding out. For example, fiscal expansion, to the extent that it increases income, will generate additional private sector saving which can be used for private investment meaning that the crowding out is less. Since our interest is in the direction of the offsetting effects of fiscal changes rather than their magnitude, the assumption of full employment yields the desired end.

F. Suppose All International Transactions Were Carried out Using Dollars

In the analysis above, changes in the exchange rate played an important role in coming to a conclusion about the efficacy of public policy choices. When the changes were considered, they frequently reversed the conclusions drawn as to the cause of the trade deficit. Would this be altered if the transactions, both for exports and imports, were carried out in terms of dollars? Let us say, for example, that a foreign country begins to subsidize goods that it exports to the United States and Americans respond by shifting from domestically produced substitutes to the now cheaper imports paid for by giving dollars to the foreign sellers. That is, the transaction does not involve the foreign exchange market. Notice that initially imports were not paid for by additional exports since the dollar did not depreciate as it did in the preceding examples. Thus, the goods and services did not pay for goods and services. Rather, the transfer of dollars (either currency or a bank deposit) from buyer to seller is, in fact, a capital movement. Thus, the additional imports were paid for by

98

transferring the ownership of an American asset to a foreigner. What happens to the dollars transferred abroad? The foreign owner can either use them to buy American goods and services or sell them to some other non-American for the same purpose. When this is done, goods and services exported will then pay for goods and services imported. When the adjustment process is completed, the American import competing industries will be adversely affected while the export industries will be favorably affected. The same result will obtain as if the transaction had gone through the foreign exchange market.

About the Author

Gail Makinen's professional life has been divided into two almost equal 25-year periods, one academic, the other as a professional adviser to the U.S. Congress. The academic portion consisted of appointments at the University of Michigan (Dearborn), Wayne State University (tenured), George Mason University, and the last 11 years of his working life at Georgetown University's McCourt School of Public Policy. His teaching consisted primarily of courses in monetary economics, international trade and finance, and macroeconomics. During this period, he authored or co-authored more than 30 articles in peer-reviewed academic journals, including the *American Economic Review*, the *Journal of Political Economy*, the *Journal of Business*, and the *Journal of Finance*. Several of the articles have been republished in books of readings and as case studies in popularly used economic text books. One has garnered more than 100 citations and another received the Jesse Burkhead Award for one of the two best articles published in the *Public Budgeting and Finance* (2001). He has also written entries in several economic encyclopedias. In addition to his journal articles, he has published seven books (several co-authored), the two most recent of which are *Studies in Hyperinflation & Stabilization* (2014), the foreword of which is written by Thomas Sargent, the 2011 recipient of the Nobel Prize in Economics, and *Essays on Money and Public Debt* (2019).

For 25 years, Dr. Makinen served as a nonpartisan economic adviser to Congress in his role as Principal Macroeconomist for the Government Accountability Office and, later, as Specialist in Economic Policy for the Congressional Research Service (a part of the Library of Congress). In addition to supporting individual members of Congress, his work was primarily with the Senate committees on Banking and Finance and the House committee on Banking and Financial Services (mainly its subcommittee on Domestic and International Monetary Policy), the House Budget Committee and the Joint Economic Committee. In his role as adviser, he gave briefings to Congressional staffs and members of Congress, prepared background studies and special reports in his areas of expertise, assisted Congressional staff in organizing hearing, suggesting witnesses who would be called to offer testimony before these committees, assisted staff members in preparing questions that members might ask the experts, testifying himself before committees, etc.

Dr. Makinen received his B.S. in Business Administration (summa cum laude) from Central Michigan University and his M.A. and Ph.D. in economics from Wayne State University.